# WOLVERHAMPTON WANDERERS CHAMPIONS

## 1953/54

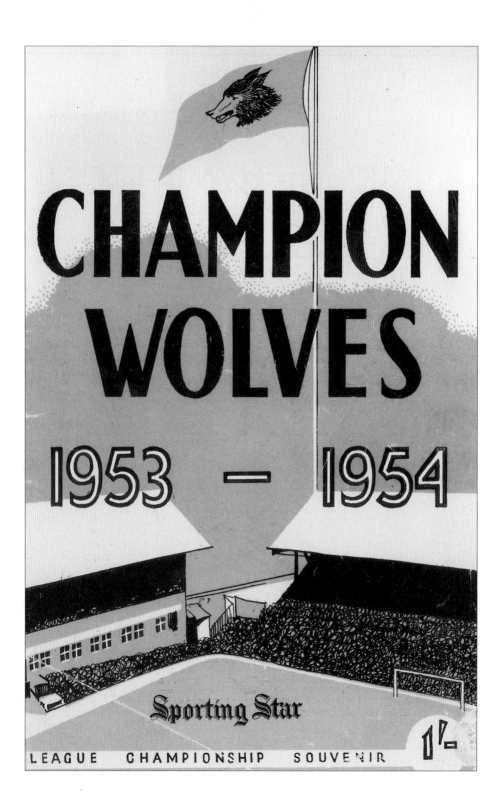

# WOLVERHAMPTON WANDERERS CHAMPIONS

## 1953 / 54

JOHN SHIPLEY

TEMPUS

*This book is dedicated to my wife, Kate. Also to all Wolves' players, past and present.*
*My sincere best wishes to all those who are involved with or who are addicted to 'The Wolves'.*
*And a special dedication to the great Dennis Wilshaw, who sadly passed away earlier this year.*

*Frontispiece:* Champion Wolves souvenir brochure.

First published 2004

Tempus Publishing Limited
The Mill, Brimscombe Port,
Stroud, Gloucestershire, GL5 2QG
www.tempus-publishing.com

© John Shipley, 2004

The right of John Shipley to be identified as the Author
of this work has been asserted in accordance with the
Copyrights, Designs and Patents Act 1988.

British Library Cataloguing in Publication Data.
A catalogue record for this book is available from the British Library.

ISBN 0 7524 3234 6

Typesetting and origination by Tempus Publishing Limited
Printed and bound in Great Britain

# Acknowledgements

I would like to say a big thank you to the following people for the assistance they have given to me during the production of this book. In particular to James Howarth and everyone at Tempus Publishing Group, without whom this book may not have ever been finished.

My eternal gratitude to Mel Eves for his invaluable help with this project.

A huge extra-special thank you to Wolverhampton Wanderers Football Club for putting up with my questions and allowing me to look at, photograph and reproduce artefacts and memorabilia in this homage to Wolves. In particular, my thanks go to Wolves' archivist Graham Hughes for his kindness and assistance with this project. To the directors, management, players and staff at Wolverhampton Wanderers. To everyone and anyone who has ever written about the Wolves.

To everyone who has helped me with proof-reading or has loaned Wolves memorabilia: my long-suffering wife Kate, my sons John and Peter, Ray Whitehouse, and Ron Hollingworth and the Hollingworth family.

Thanks also go to: Ben Smallman, the *Bridgnorth Journal*, Charles Ross at ALOB, the *Shropshire Star* and its sister newspaper the *Express & Star* and the *Birmingham Post & Mail* Ltd.

My gratitude also goes to the staff at: the Birmingham City Library, Archives and Local Studies service and the British Association of Picture Libraries and Agencies (BAPLA) and the Wolverhampton archives amd local studies services.

Photographic and other acknowledgements: While every effort has been made to trace and acknowledge all copyright holders, we apologise for any errors or omissions. The author wishes to thank and acknowledge the following for providing photographs and for permission to reproduce copyright material: Ron Hollingworth and the Hollingworth family, Graham Hughes plus the directors, management, players and staff at Wolverhampton Wanderers for supplying a few photographs, Mel Eves, Geoff Allman and Empics.

*John K. Shipley*
*Spring 2004*

# List of Matches

All games are Football League Division One unless otherwise stated.

| | |
|---|---|
| 19 August 1953 | Burnley 4 *v*. Wolves 1 |
| 22 August 1953 | Manchester City 0 *v*. Wolves 4 |
| 26 August 1953 | Sunderland 3 *v*. Wolves 2 |
| 29 August 1953 | Wolves 3 *v*. Cardiff City 1 |
| 31 August 1953 | Wolves 3 *v*. Sunderland 1 |
| 5 September 1953 | Arsenal 2 *v*. Wolves 3 |
| 7 September 1953 | Wolves 2 *v*. Liverpool 1 |
| 12 September 1953 | Wolves 4 *v*. Portsmouth 3 |
| 16 September 1953 | Liverpool 1 *v*. Wolves 1 |
| 19 September 1953 | Blackpool 0 *v*. Wolves 0 |
| 26 September 1953 | Wolves 8 *v*. Chelsea 1 |
| 30 September 1953 | Wolves 3 *v*. South Africa 1 (Floodlit Friendly) |
| 3 October 1953 | Sheffield United 3 *v*. Wolves 3 |
| 10 October 1953 | Newcastle United 1 *v*. Wolves 2 |
| 14 October 1953 | Wolves 2 *v*. Glasgow Celtic 0 (Floodlit Friendly) |
| 17 October 1953 | Wolves 3 *v*. Manchester United 1 |
| 24 October 1953 | Bolton Wanderers 1 *v*. Wolves 1 |
| 31 October 1953 | Wolves 1 *v*. Preston North End 0 |
| 7 November 1953 | Middlesbrough 3 *v*. Wolves 3 |
| 14 November 1953 | Wolves 1 *v*. West Bromwich Albion 0 |
| 21 November 1953 | Charlton Athletic 0 *v*. Wolves 2 |
| 28 November 1953 | Wolves 4 *v*. Sheffield Wednesday 1 |
| 5 December 1953 | Tottenham Hotspur 2 *v*. Wolves 3 |
| 12 December 1953 | Wolves 1 *v*. Burnley 2 |
| 19 December 1953 | Wolves 3 *v*. Manchester City 1 |
| 24 December 1953 | Wolves 1 *v*. Aston Villa 2 |
| 26 December 1953 | Aston Villa 1 *v*. Wolves 2 |
| 2 January 1954 | Cardiff City 1 *v*. Wolves 3 |
| 9 January 1954 | Wolves 1 *v*. Birmingham City 2 (FA Cup Round Three) |

| | |
|---|---|
| 16 January 1954 | Wolves 0 v. Arsenal 2 |
| 23 January 1954 | Portsmouth 2 v. Wolves 0 |
| 6 February 1954 | Wolves 4 v. Blackpool Town 1 |
| 13 February 1954 | Chelsea 4 v. Wolves 2 |
| 20 February 1954 | Wolves 6 v. Sheffield United 1 |
| 27 February 1954 | Wolves 3 v. Newcastle United 2 |
| 6 March 1954 | Manchester United 1 v. Wolves 0 |
| 10 March 1954 | Wolves 3 v. Racing Club Of Buenos Aires 1 (Floodlit Friendly) |
| 20 March 1954 | Preston North End 0 v. Wolves 1 |
| 24 March 1954 | Wolves 1 v. Bolton Wanderers 1 |
| 27 March 1954 | Wolves 2 v. Middlesbrough 4 |
| 3 April 1954 | West Bromwich Albion 0 v. Wolves 1 |
| 10 April 1954 | Wolves 5 v. Charlton Athletic 0 |
| 17 April 1954 | Sheffield Wednesday 0 v. Wolves 0 |
| 19 April 1954 | Wolves 4 v. Huddersfield Town 0 |
| 20 April 1954 | Huddersfield Town 2 v. Wolves 1 |
| 24 April 1954 | Wolves 2 v. Tottenham Hotspur 0 |

Wolves' manager, Stan Cullis.

Joe Gardiner.

# Introduction

The fiftieth anniversary of Wolves' first ever League Championship was officially marked on 24 April 2004. A momentous and pioneering milestone in the history of the club that needs to be both remembered and celebrated by every true fan of Wolverhampton Wanderers. My sincere wish is that by stirring memories of Wolves' great golden age this book will to do just that.

To serve as a taster to Wolves' first League Championship, and to enable those readers less familiar with this epic achievement, I have included a brief history of the club and their many Championship near misses. My aim was to capture the true spirit of the time, and thus convey the depth of the pride and passion felt by Wolves and their fans in winning the League title in 1953/54.

In 1877, St Luke's School, Blakenhall formed a football team which, two years later, amalgamated with Blakenhall Wanderers Cricket Club to become Wolverhampton Wanderers Football Club. Eleven years later, Wolves, as they had come to be known, were one of the original twelve members of the Football League along with Accrington, Aston Villa, Blackburn Rovers, Bolton Wanderers, Burnley, Derby County, Everton, Notts County, Preston North End, Stoke and West Bromwich Albion. Wolves finished in third place behind Champions Preston and runners-up Aston Villa in that first ever season of League football 1888/89.

Before 1950, Wolves, as they are famously known throughout the world, won the FA Cup three times, in 1892/93, 1907/08 and 1948/49, and were runners-up on four other occasions, 1888/89, 1895/96, 1920/21 and 1938/39. Wolves were also Second Division champions in 1931/32, and Third Division (North) champions in 1923/24. In other words, the club had won every major domestic honour in the game bar one, the big one – the League Championship. In the six and a half decades since the formation of the Football League, success in only this one competition had managed to elude them.

They had come mighty close on a number of occasions, the closest in 1949/50, when they finished second behind Portsmouth. The most galling part of this achievement was that both teams had managed to amass 53 points. Wolves only lost out to Pompey because of their inferior goal average: despite scoring 2 goals more than their South-Coast rivals they had unfortunately managed to concede 11 more.

However, this wasn't the first time Wolves had been the bridesmaid and not the bride. Under the guidance of the legendary Major Frank Buckley, they had finished in second place on two previous occasions, oddly enough in consecutive seasons: in 1937/38, 1 point behind Arsenal, and in 1938/39, 4 points behind Everton.

Would the wonderfully talented 'Buckley Babes' have eventually made it into pole position? We'll never know, because the Second World War intervened, putting to an end all the fanciful 'what-if' speculation.

Actually, with a little more luck, the 1938/39 season might have gone down as a landmark in footballing history, as second-in-the-League Wolves also reached the FA Cup final. According to popular opinion (including, it seemed, every newspaper reporter in the land apart from those in South Hampshire) their opponents, Portsmouth, had more chance of plaiting fog than beating Wolves! It seemed that Wolves had only to turn up to collect the trophy – Portsmouth were not given a prayer. Funny old game, isn't it? On the day, Wolves lost 4-1 to a team that finished only 5 points off the relegation spot. Had Wolves finished first in both competitions instead of second, they would have become the first club in the modern game to win the coveted League and Cup double.

The details of Wolves' three second-place finishes in the First Division are:

**1937/38**

|            | PLD | W  | D  | L  | F  | A  | PTS |
|------------|-----|----|----|----|----|----|-----|
| Arsenal    | 42  | 21 | 10 | 11 | 77 | 44 | 52  |
| **Wolves** | 42  | 20 | 11 | 11 | 72 | 49 | 51  |

**1938/39**

|            | PLD | W  | D  | L  | F  | A  | PTS |
|------------|-----|----|----|----|----|----|-----|
| Everton    | 42  | 27 | 5  | 10 | 88 | 52 | 59  |
| **Wolves** | 42  | 22 | 11 | 9  | 88 | 39 | 55  |

**1949/50**

|             | PLD | W  | D  | L  | F  | A  | PTS |
|-------------|-----|----|----|----|----|----|-----|
| Portsmouth  | 42  | 22 | 9  | 11 | 74 | 38 | 53  |
| **Wolves**  | 42  | 20 | 13 | 9  | 76 | 49 | 53  |

Wolves' fortunes had taken a turn for the worse when they were relegated from the First Division at the end of the 1905/06 season, a dim period in their history that saw them languish in the Second Division for over two decades, apart from one season in the Third Division (North). The directors knew that something had to be done. The revitalisation of Wolves' fortunes started on 27 June 1927, when Second Division Wolverhampton Wanderers appointed Major Frank Buckley to the post of manager/secretary, replacing the dismissed previous incumbent Fred Scotchbrook on a three-year contract. He stayed until March 1944, a tenure of almost seventeen years, during which time he became known as the 'Master of Molineux', indisputably exerting a major influence on the club and shaping it to suit his own style. Buckley arrived at Wolves at a time when the club was desperately short of money and going nowhere fast.

It took Buckley four seasons to establish a decent team, which in 1930/31 he guided to fourth place in the Second Division. The following season, 1931/32, Wolves won the Second Division Championship, and now once again the Major set about building a team that would be strong enough to compete with the best sides and challenge for top honours. Sadly, the outbreak of war halted Wolves' revival, but the groundwork had been done. In his time, Buckley brought to the club and developed some great players, household names for all Wolves' fans. A number of them became Wolves legends: Stan Cullis, Dennis Westcott, Billy Wright, Jimmy Mullen, Dennis

Wilshaw, Dicky Dorsett, Tom Galley, Joe Gardiner, Billy Hartill, Reg Hollingworth and Bryn Jones to name but a few.

In 1938 Buckley's contract had been renewed for another ten years, but in March 1944 he sensationally quit, citing private and personal matters as the reason; maybe we'll never know the real truth of what happened, and why he decided to leave the club he loved at such a moment. After leaving Wolves, he went to manage Notts County, Hull City and Leeds United, during which time he signed the legendary genial Welsh giant John Charles for the club, and finally Walsall Town from April 1953 to September 1955. He retired from the game at the ripe old age of seventy-one, having never been able to repeat the success he'd had with Wolves. Surprisingly, under Buckley's tutelage Wolves won only one trophy, the 1942 Wartime Cup.

After Buckley left in 1944, Wolves' directors hired the experienced Ted Vizard to manage the club. Ted Vizard had a distinguished playing career, capped 22 times for Wales and winning the FA Cup on two occasions with Bolton Wanderers. Vizard's Wolves team included many stars, and one of the brightest was the great Stanley Cullis.

Season 1946/47 heralded the resumption of first-class football after the end of the Second World War, and that year, Wolves were disappointed to finish third in the First Division with the same number of points as second-placed Manchester United and only 1 behind Champions Liverpool. So near yet so far, once again.

Then in May 1947, Stan Cullis surprised many fans and commentators when, at the relatively young age of thirty-one, he announced his retirement from playing to become assistant manager to Ted Vizard. He took over the manager's reins in June 1948, when Vizard resigned. Cullis was a tough, uncompromising and inspirational manager who was to steer Wolves to the most successful period in their history. By the time Cullis played out his final season as a player, a number of future stars had already begun to establish themselves in the first team: goalkeeper Bert Williams, full-backs Gus McLean and Billy Crook, half-back Billy Wright, and forwards Johnny Hancocks, Jesse Pye and Jimmy Mullen. These players, plus older stars Tom Galley and Dennis Westcott, began to gel as a class act, earning Wolves an awesome reputation as a fast, attacking team that neither asked for or gave quarter.

In 1947/48, with new boys Roy Pritchard, Bill Shorthouse, Jimmy Dunn and Sammy Smyth in the side, Wolves ended the season in fifth spot. A year later in 1948/49 they reached sixth position, also winning the FA Cup, beating Leicester 3-1; not bad for Cullis' first season as a manager. Wolves' team at Wembley was Williams; Pritchard, Springthorpe; Crook, Shorthouse, Wright; Hancocks, Smyth, Pye, Dunn, Mullen. Then came the depressing second-place finish in 1949/50. Following this disappointment, and judged against their own high standards, over the course of the next two seasons Wolves' form dipped considerably, falling to fourteenth position in 1950/51, and in 1951/52 ending the season in sixteenth spot to typify Wolves' two seasons of relative mediocrity before once again getting their act together for another go at reaching the top spot.

It was during the early 1950s that Cullis was beavering away to build another top-class side upon the backbone of the good team that he had inherited from Major Buckley and Ted Vizard. In came Roy Swinbourne, Dennis Wilshaw, Bill Slater and Peter Broadbent as Cullis sought to find the best permutation of players, blending the talent at his disposal into a team of winners. In doing this, he also created a behind-the-first-eleven outfit, Wolves reserves, a team that would have given many a First-Division outfit a run for its money.

The following season, 1952/53, saw a resurgence of Wolves' fortunes as they once again claimed third place. This time they finished 3 points behind Champions Arsenal and Tom Finney's Preston North End, who both finished on 54 points. Arsenal won the title by virtue of having a better goal average than the Lilywhites. We didn't know it at the time, but this battling third place was to provide the springboard for Wolves' first Championship in the following season.

Up till then, in ten seasons, excluding the war break, Wolves had finished second three times, third twice, had two fifth and one sixth placing, and won the FA Cup once, to earn the recognition as being among the top clubs in the country.

So now the stage was set for Stan Cullis and his happy Wanderers to launch their 1953/54 assault on the biggest prize in English football, and as we know, they did it – League Champions 1953/54: Wolverhampton Wanderers.

This book is a history of that memorable 1953/54 season, and the unique race for the title between the two best sides in the country, ironically both from the Black Country: Wolverhampton Wanderers and their closest rivals West Bromwich Albion.

Black Country people are intensely loyal to their homeland and proud of their heritage, and fifty years ago, their pride and passion was at chest-bursting proportions as the region's two top football teams went head to head in the race for the nation's premier honours.

1953/54 was the season that both clubs won a top honour; Wolves the League Championship and Albion the FA Cup.

Writing this book has given me a lot of pleasure; I hope you enjoy reading it.

With every best wish,

John Shipley
Lifelong Wolves fanatic

# 1953/54 and all that

Thank goodness early-season form is never a good indicator of what might be achieved over a whole season. After all, the League campaign is a marathon rather than a sprint, spread as it was in those days over forty-two games; and a good job too!

In their infinite wisdom, the Football League decided to move the League fixtures that were originally scheduled to have been played on Saturday 1 May 1954 to midweek in August 1953. The reason given for the change was the BBC had decided to broadcast the FA Cup final, scheduled for 1 May 1954, live to the nation. The League deemed it not fair to broadcast one specific match while League matches were in progress. To ensure that there could be no misunderstanding, the official explanation went something like this: 'In order that all but the two teams engaged in the FA Cup final will have a free day on 1 May next year'. Clear as mud!

This fixture rearrangement meant that Wolves would begin their onslaught on the 1953/54 First Division title away to Burnley at Turf Moor on Wednesday 19 August 1953. They were blasted 4-1. Was this season going to be another failure for the boys in old gold and black? No, of course it wasn't! However, let's get back to 1953, because before the season began in earnest, there were one or two games to get out of the way first.

As part of their pre-season warm up, Wolves travelled to Edinburgh to play a charity game against a combined Hibernian and Hearts eleven at Easter Road on Saturday 1 August 1953. It was the summer bank holiday weekend, and Britain was enjoying a marvellous spell of excellent weather. The game kicked off in heatwave conditions, with Wolves intent on a good start; and they got their wish in the first minute as Dennis Wilshaw swept them into the lead. Unfortunately, the Scots hadn't read the script and hit back, eventually running out 3-2 winners. Roy Swinbourne headed Wolves' second goal in the 56th minute. Not the best of starts, and not the best match ever seen at Hibs' ground. Mind you, there's no doubt that the crippling heat took its toll on the players.

Wolves moved the annual charity practice match from its normal Saturday to Wednesday 12 August because of the impending midweek start to the season. The match kicked off at Molineux at 6.45 p.m. in the hope that a few more fans would turn up to watch what was usually a good game of football; 9,173 of the faithful were treated to some excellent play by both sides, and raised £418 14s, not much by today's standards, but a fortune then. The Colours beat the Whites 3-1, Peter Broadbent opening the scoring for the Whites in the 36th minute for what was a very short lead; 1 minute later Roy Swinbourne equalised for the Colours. A Dennis Wilshaw goal either side of half-time wrapped it up for the first eleven.

**Colours:** Sims; Short, Pritchard; W.J. Slater, Shorthouse, Wright; Hancocks, Stockin, Swinbourne, Wilshaw, Mullen.

**Whites:** Williams; Gibbons, Guttridge (replaced at half-time by Clamp); Chatham. Stuart, Baxter; Smith, Broadbent, Taylor, Mason, Clews.

**Referee:** Mr F. Read (Willenhall)

Billy Wright was chosen to lead a Birmingham County FA eleven to Hamburg for a game against a select Hamburg eleven to mark the opening of the new Volksparkstation stadium on Sunday 16 August 1953. The Hamburgers took a 2-0 lead before being pegged back to 2-2 with goals from Ronnie Allen and Roy Swinbourne. Gil Merrick saved a penalty but couldn't prevent the Germans from grabbing the winner, as Hamburg ran out 3-2 victors. The playing of this game was an interesting fixture decision considering there were only a few days to go before the start of the season proper.

Birmingham County FA Squad: Merrick (Birmingham City); Parkes (Aston Villa), Green (Birmingham City); Boyd (Birmingham City), Kirk (Coventry City), Wright (Wolves) (Capt.); Griffin (WBA), Ryan (WBA), Swinbourne (Wolves), Murphy (Birmingham City), Lockhart (Aston Villa). Reserve: Allen (WBA).

At 2.52 p.m. on the day prior to Wolves' game at Turf Moor came the news that every English cricket fan craved to hear, as crowds invaded the pitch at The Oval after England, led by Yorkshireman Len Hutton, beat Australia to win the Ashes for the first time in twenty-nine years. England had begun the day needing 94 runs to win, and lost Peter May to an excellent delivery before he could get near his half-century, bringing the Middlesex pair of Bill Edrich and Dennis Compton together at the wicket. The pair set about the Australian attack with real vigour, and suddenly England only required 4 runs to win. Morris took the ball for the next over with the crowd urging Compton to hit him for four. This he promptly did with his trademark leg-sweep. As the ball hit the boundary fence, most of the 30,000 crowd engulfed their heroes as they left the field, ending twenty years of Australian domination – fantastic.

Meanwhile, up in Lancashire Wolves had a League game to play.

Wolves' skipper Billy Wright and colleagues proudly show off their haul of trophies. Left to right: Bill Shorthouse, Joe Gardiner, Billy Wright, George Poyser and George Palmer.

# BURNLEY V. WOLVES

**Football League Division One at Turf Moor**

**Date:** Wednesday 19 August 1953          **Attendance:** 32,922

Wolves had lost the final game of the 1952/53 season 3-2 to Tottenham at White Hart Lane, so I guess you could say that the expectations of Wolves' fans were not exactly burning brightly; more like smouldering a bit. The corresponding game of the previous season at Burnley had ended all square at 0-0; surely Wolves could do better this time?

Almost 33,000 turned out on a bright summer day in Lancashire to watch this encounter. However, despite the sunshine the pitch was slick and slippery after a good deal of rain.

It was strange to be playing the opening match of the season in the middle of the week. Stan Cullis had selected Nigel Sims in goal in place of Bert Williams and Ronnie Stockin at inside right; there was no place for star playmaker Peter Broadbent.

Wolves started extremely well, passing the ball around the wide open spaces of the Turf Moor pitch, and went ahead after only 1 minute 50 seconds when Roy Swinbourne swooped to fire the ball home; definitely a contender for the first goal of the season. Wolves followed up with wave after wave of dangerous attacks, completely bossing the middle of the park. Surely it was only a matter of time before the second goal went in, such was Wolves' domination of the game. Unfortunately it didn't. Successive attacks were either repulsed or chances to score were squandered. Half-time came with the score still 1-0 in Wolves' favour, so things were still looking pretty good.

After the interval, Wolves really should have wrapped up the game, but as time progressed, so the danger increased. It was the last half-hour of the second half that was to prove a disaster for the visitors, as Burnley turned up the volume, succeeding where Wolves had failed and driven on by Jimmy Adamson and Jimmy McIlroy.

Now followed 2 minutes of defensive madness on the part of Wolves. On 62 minutes, inside left Les Shannon raced through to bring the scores level with a firm shot that took a wicked deflection off a Wolves' foot. Then, 2 minutes later, Burnley went into the lead through centre forward Bill Holden. Now, Wolves found themselves having to defend in numbers as the Clarets began to win the midfield battle. With the visitors' defence at sixes and sevens, Brian Pilkington pounced on a 70th minute mistake by Bill Shorthouse as he uncharacteristically dithered on the ball, allowing Holden to easily rob him before sliding his pass to the young left-winger, who made it 3-1 to the home side to emphasize an amazing transformation. Six minutes from time Shannon wrapped it up for Burnley with his second goal after he cleverly sprang Wolves' offside trap. Gray sent through a hopeful ball, and Wolves' defence almost froze in anticipation of a sharp blast from the referee's whistle, but the linesman unfortunately kept his flag down.

**Burnley 4**
  *Shannon 2 (62 and 84)*
  *Holden (64)*
  *Pilkington (70)*

**Wolves 1**
  *Swinbourne (2)*

14

Wolves' playing and coaching staff.

So that was it, 4-1 in a game of two contrasting halves. Prior to the interval, Wolves had showed that they could create chances, and suggested that on another day they were capable of scoring a lot of goals. Hancocks and Mullen looked menacing on the flanks, delivering many dangerous crosses, while Swinbourne looked powerful in the centre of Wolves' attack. Certainly the silky skills of Peter Broadbent were missed, but Wolves had had chance to get used to this, having been forced to play without the talented inside forward since the previous season's 5-3 defeat at Arsenal on 17 January. Burnley's fast-running forwards had exposed a number of weaknesses in Wolves' defence that required a little tightening up: it's no good scoring goals if you let more in than the other team.

Wolves had only a couple of days to work on this aspect of their game before it was to be put to the test once again. Having said that, Billy Wright produced his customary immaculate performance and, apart from his costly error, Bill Shorthouse did well. Sadly Wilshaw and Stockin faded badly in the second half, exposing Wright and Slater to tremendous pressure from the home side.

Not too good a start for Wolves, you might say. Back in the Black Country, Albion beat reigning Champions Arsenal 2-0 at The Hawthorns with both goals from Johnny Nicholls. Next up for the Wanderers were Manchester City, again away.

---

**Burnley:** Thompson; Aird, Winton; Adamson, Cummings, Rudman; Gray, McIlroy, Holden, Shannon, Pilkington

**Wolves:** Sims; Short, Pritchard; W.J. Slater, Shorthouse, Wright; Hancocks, Stockin, Swinbourne, Wilshaw, Mullen

# MANCHESTER CITY v. WOLVES

Football League Division One at Maine Road

**Date:** Saturday 22 August 1953          **Attendance:** 20,039

Was it something about playing on Saturday? Whatever it was, Wolves' fans loved it. Two goals for Roy Swinbourne, plus one each for Bill Slater and Dennis Wilshaw, saw Wolves cruise to a deserved victory in front of just over 20,000 people.

Cullis decided against making wholesale changes and sent out the same eleven players for this second game of the season. Facing them in goal for City was the great Bert Trautmann, and adding to this formidable human barrier was the memory of the previous season's 3-1 defeat.

Wolves began the game with an assault on the City goal, which happily this time they kept up for the entire game; it didn't take them long to chalk up a goal. Three minutes after the quarter-hour mark Dennis Wilshaw banged home a good shot to give Wolves the lead. Wanderers were moving the ball around the pitch beautifully, but amazingly it took them another 18 minutes to fashion a second. This time it was the superb Bill Slater who scored a neat goal in the 36th minute. It was 2-0 at half-time and looking good for Wolves.

Unlike the game at Turf Moor, this time Wolves came out for the second half showing exactly the same determination as they had in the first period. They went 3-0 up in the 56th minute with an excellently taken goal from Roy Swinbourne, before having two goals harshly ruled out by the match officials; first it was Wilshaw for offside and then Wright for a foul, both disallowed by the referee, and both seemingly incorrect decisions. On the heels of these incidents, City right-back Branagan appeared to fist the ball off his own goal line; it looked like a penalty, but the referee was having none of it. It began to look as though the officials might have had a bet on City; they were certainly favouring the home side with their decisions. However, ultimately even they couldn't stop Wolves.

In the 83rd minute up popped Swinbourne to make it 4-0 to the visitors, bringing boos of derision from the home supporters. Apart from one or two individuals, City were simply outclassed. Their too-often frail defence in front of German goalkeeper Bert Trautmann was powerless to halt Wolves' display of aggressive attacking. Even the undisputed guile of future Leeds and England boss Don Revie coupled with the power of John Williamson and Ivor Broadis failed to prevent this emphatic Wolves victory. To be fair City did try, and Nigel Sims in Wolves' goal had to be on his toes to keep out a number of good efforts, handling the greasy ball very competently. In the end, City could consider themselves lucky that, even with the help of the ref and his mates, they had somehow kept the score to 4-0, as tempestuous Wolves could and should have scored more. A pleasing aspect for Wolves fans was that the entire team had worked tremendously hard throughout the 90 minutes, thoroughly deserving their victory.

**Wolves 4**                                        Manchester City 0

*Wilshaw (18)*
*W.J. Slater (36)*
*Swinbourne 2 (56 and 83)*

16

# MANCHESTER CITY v. WOLVES

Dennis Wilshaw, Wolves.

West Brom slipped up at home, only taking one point in a 1-1 draw with Bolton Wanderers; Ray Barlow getting his first Baggies goal of the season. After two games the League table was being topped by Sheffield Wednesday, closely followed by Charlton Athletic, and their Sheffield United rivals in third spot. Albion were fourth with 3 points and Wolves, unlucky for some, in thirteenth place with 2; but there was still a lot of football to be played yet.

Oh no! The next game would be played on 'bad-luck' Wednesday.

---

**Manchester City:** Trautmann; Branagan, Hannaway; Revie, Ewing, Paul; Anders, Hart, Williamson, Broadis, Clarke

**Wolves:** Sims; Short, Pritchard; W.J. Slater, Shorthouse, Wright; Hancocks, Stockin, Swinbourne, Wilshaw, Mullen

# Sunderland v. Wolves

Football League Division One at Roker Park

**Date:** Wednesday 26 August 1953          **Attendance:** 57,135

Over 57,000 Wearsiders crammed into Roker to witness this pulsating game between two sides committed to attack. However, the historical omens weren't good, because Wolves hadn't won there since Christmas Day 1946. They had either lost or drawn, and the previous season's result had been a 5-2 thrashing. Hopefully, this time Wolves would do better. Sunderland's expensively assembled and star-studded team, reputedly costing £150,000, included the great Trevor Ford at centre forward and the immensely talented clown-prince of English soccer Len Shackleton. Fans could be excused for being a little confused at times with three Wrights on the pitch, two for the home side and one for Wolves.

Once again, Wolves began like an express train, putting the Black Cats firmly on the back foot, but unfortunately, chance after chance went a-begging. As early as the 3rd minute, Ronnie Stockin missed a great opportunity to score. The inside right found himself in acres of space, but he spooned his hurried shot high into the crowd. Then Wilshaw forced his way through the Sunderland defence only to put his shot wide of the mark.

So dominant in the opening quarter of an hour were Wolves that it would have been understandable if they had allowed their heads to drop when much against the run of play Sunderland hit them with the old one-two. First, it was Tommy Wright on 18 minutes who deflected Arthur Wright's shot into Wolves' net. Then 6 minutes later Len Shackleton repeated the punishment, doubling Wolves' bad luck as once again the ball was deflected past the helpless Nigel Sims. This time Bill Slater was the culprit, when it looked odds on that Roy Pritchard on Wolves' goal line would clear easily. It stayed 2-0 at the break. What would Cullis be able to do?

Shorthouse was maintaining a firm grip on Trevor Ford, but 7 minutes after the turn-round Wolves' determination was dealt yet another body-blow when right-back Stelling took the ball away from Mullen all too easily and his pass found Aitken, who quickly moved the ball on to Kirtley. The winger tore down the right flank before centring. His cross on the run was well controlled by the burly Welsh centre forward who crashed home a stunning shot for Sunderland's third. It couldn't be said that Wolves renewed their attacking, because they had never stopped.

A little bit of luck finally came Wolves' way 5 minutes later when Dennis Wilshaw was brought down in the penalty area. Up stepped ace penalty-taker Johnny Hancocks to crack the ball past Cowan: a glimmer of hope? The bad news was that Lady Luck's appearance proved to be only temporary. Jimmy Mullen watched his excellent effort scrape the wrong side of the bar, and a little later Roy Swinbourne hooked a shot narrowly wide. In the 81st minute Wilshaw headed a second for Wolves. Billy Wright lobbed a high ball into the Sunderland penalty area, which Swinbourne

---

**Sunderland 3**

*Wright (T) (18)*

*Shackleton (24)*

*Ford (52)*

**Wolves 2**

*Hancocks penalty (57)*

*Wilshaw (81)*

Trevor Ford, Sunderland.

headed down for Wilshaw to score from close range. Wolves piled on the pressure, seeking the equaliser and went close through Hancocks, Swinbourne and Wilshaw, but it was a case of too little too late as Sunderland's defenders just about managed to keep out the ferocious Wolves attackers.

In a nutshell, the story of the game was that the home side's forwards had taken their chances better than Wolves, something else for Cullis and his team to work on. The faithful prayed that the players were fast learners.

Wolves were playing well, but just needed a bit of extra umph. So far, three games played (although all three away from home) had resulted in one win and two defeats; still it could have been worse!

Albion's first away game was a triumphant 3-1 win over Manchester United at Old Trafford, with goals from Jimmy Dudley, Johnny Nicholls and George Lee. However, it was Huddersfield Town that now occupied the League's top spot; Wolves had slipped to sixteenth.

Now at least the majority of Wolves' supporters would be able to see their team play, because the next two games would be at Molineux. Actually, the defeat at Sunderland might have been a blessing in disguise because it was to herald the start of an 18-match unbeaten run for Wolves.

---

**Sunderland:** Cowan; Stelling, Hedley; Aitken, Daniel, Wright (A); Wright (T), Kirtley, Ford, Shackleton, McSeveney

**Wolves:** Sims; Short, Pritchard; W.J. Slater, Shorthouse, Wright; Hancocks, Stockin, Swinbourne, Wilshaw, Mullen

# WOLVES V. CARDIFF CITY

**Football League Division One at Molineux**

**Date:** Saturday 29 August 1953          **Attendance:** 35,221

---

At last, a home game, and versus a team that Wolves quite often did well against (in 1952/53 Cardiff had been beaten 1-0). This was much better; a crowd of 35,221 watched intently as Wolves swung smoothly into gear with goals from Johnny Hancocks, Jimmy Mullen and Dennis Wilshaw.

Cullis made the first change of the season, which was actually the first in sixteen games. Happily for many fans, RAF player Peter Broadbent was drafted in for his first start, Ron Stockin making way for him. Broadbent hadn't played since the 5-2 defeat at Arsenal on 17 January the previous season when Wolves had finished a creditable third in the League.

Almost unbelievably in a game that saw Wolves throw everything at Cardiff but the kitchen sink, the visitors scored first. Unlucky for some, and particularly for Wolves, on the 13th minute mark, Howells threw the ball out to centre forward Wilf Grant, who waltzed his way through Wolves' defence to beat Nigel Sims with a smart shot.

Wolves now pounded the Welshmen's goal with renewed vigour, but it took them 20 minutes to get their scoring act together, eventually getting their just rewards in the 33rd minute through Mr Reliable, Dennis Wilshaw. It took only another 5 minutes for Wolves to make it 2-1, Jimmy Mullen meeting a perfect Hancocks cross at the far post to head home superbly. Next it was Hancocks' turn to score, again from the penalty spot; his second in successive games. The little winger gave fans the horrors by slipping on his run-up; they needn't have worried because he still managed to wallop the ball into the net. The score remained 3-1 at the break.

The fans anticipated a goal-fest in the second half, and but for the brave efforts of goalkeeper Howells, ably backed up by Sherwood and his fellow defenders, Wolves' goal tally might well have ended up closer to ten. When the referee blew his whistle, every Wolves' fan applauded what had been a superb performance; even a goal-less second half couldn't diminish their appreciation of a job well done. The lads had literally bombarded the Welshmen's goal from start to finish, with no prisoners being taken at any stage of the match.

Having said all of that, Cardiff chucked away a couple of good chances. Wilf Grant was guilty of a glaring miss when clear through on goal; for some reason he delayed his shot, allowing the Wolves' defence to recover. Then it was Chisholm who shot wide when it looked easier to score. In goal for the Bluebirds, Howells was quite magnificent, keeping out a great many goalbound efforts. Oh, and Wolves also hit both bar and post several times.

So Wolves' first four games had yielded the somewhat disappointing tally of only 4 points; especially considering that they had scored 10 goals; the problem was that they had conceded 8.

---

**Wolves 3**                                    **Cardiff City 1**

*Wilshaw (33)*                                    *Grant (13)*

*Mullen (38)*

*Hancocks (penalty) (44)*

George Poyser shakes the hand of Peter Broadbent as his teammates look on.

Chances were being created in abundance, but not enough of them were being stuck away; also, the defence needed tightening up a lot.

Across the Black Country, West Bromwich Albion had kept up their cracking start to the season, recording their third victory in four starts, this time beating Preston 2-0 at Deepdale, Nicholls again scoring a brace. Albion now topped the League with 7 points, already 3 ahead of Wolves; Albion had scored the same number of goals as Wolves, but they'd only conceded 2.

Because of the fixture rearrangement, Wolves got a second crack at Sunderland sooner than would have been usual.

**Wolves:** Sims; Short, Pritchard; W.J. Slater, Shorthouse, Wright; Hancocks, Broadbent, Swinbourne, Wilshaw, Mullen

**Cardiff City:** Howells; Frowen, Sherwood; Hollyman. Montgomery, Sullivan; Williams (R), Harrington, Grant, Chisholm, McLoughlin

# WOLVES V. SUNDERLAND

Football League Division One at Molineux

**Date:** Monday 31 August 1953          **Attendance:** 41,442

This game, which kicked off at 6.15 p.m., provided Wolves with the opportunity to avenge the defeat at Roker Park five days earlier and, incidentally, go one better than last year's 1-1 draw. And that is exactly what they did.

For the second successive game Wolves set up a bombardment of epic proportions. However, as in previous games, this was only after they had been stung into action by their opponents. Goals from Jimmy Mullen, Roy Swinbourne and Dennis Wilshaw saw Wolves cruise home 3-1, but not before a heart-stopping scare. Inside 90 seconds Tommy Wright scored against Wolves for the second time in two games; this, one of the fastest goals ever. In this match, he was deputising for the injured Welsh international centre forward Trevor Ford.

His goal was the signal for Wolves to pile on the pressure, only for goalkeeper Cowan to prove impassable, making a string of saves to deny whirlwind Wolves. The home side should have equalised in the 10th minute when Mullen's excellent low cross was back-heeled across the box by Swinbourne. Unfortunately, no one was following up. A couple of minutes later Hancocks crossed to Mullen only for the left-winger's shot from point-blank range to be beaten away by Cowan.

On 15 minutes, Swinbourne and Broadbent narrowly failed to get on the end of another great cross from Mullen, then just after this, Hancocks screwed a blaster wide of Cowan's post. And so it continued: Broadbent skimmed the bar, Mullen headed Broadbent's cross wide then the same player hit the top of the bar with a great shot. Next, it was Swinbourne's turn to head wide, and when Cowan made a mistake by dropping the ball, the Wolves' number nine wasn't quite able to reach it. Every time the ball was passed to Hancocks and Mullen, it spelled danger for Cowan, but he somehow kept getting in the way of the ball. Surely, the big 'keeper couldn't keep a clean sheet in the face of such power? No, he couldn't. Finally, after Hancocks had again gone close a couple more times, Wolves got their reward. On 35 minutes Broadbent pushed an exquisite pass towards the Sunderland penalty area for Dennis Wilshaw to chase, winning the race against the slipping centre half Daniel and goalkeeper Cowan, who couldn't hang on to the ball as it passed him, and the Wolves number ten slotted it home as cool as you please; 1-1 at half-time.

After the break, Wolves continued where they had left off, but it wasn't until the 68th minute that they were able to grab the lead. Uncharacteristically, Cowan misjudged a well-flighted centre, only succeeding in pushing the ball to the feet of Jimmy Mullen, who made no mistake from close range. It took Wolves a mere 2 minutes to extend their lead. This time it was Roy Swinbourne who, after shrewd control of the ball, scored with a neat shot from close range following good work by Broadbent, whose return to the number eight shirt was certainly having a positive effect on Wolves'

**Wolves 3**
*Wilshaw (35)*
*Mullen (68)*
*Swinbourne (70)*

**Sunderland 1**
*Wright (T) (90 seconds)*

Peter Broadbent of Wolves.

attacking. The 41,442 crowd appreciated his inclusion in the team and his at times breathtaking skill. However, Sunderland weren't done yet, and went close a couple of times.

First, the great Len Shackleton had the crowd on its feet with a superb overhead kick that fortunately didn't go in, before Tommy Wright watched in disgust as his goalbound effort was cleared a yard from Wolves' goal line. So 3-1 it stayed, and revenge was sweet as the Wearsiders were sent packing.

On the following Wednesday, goals from Allen and Hodgkisson ensured that Albion stayed on top of the League, beating Manchester United 2-0 at The Hawthorns and putting them 3 points ahead of Wolves.

Wolves' half-back Bill Baxter and inside forward Jack Taylor both requested a transfer. Baxter stated that he was fed up with understudying Billy Wright and Bill Slater and wanted to move to a club where he would get first-team football. He had joined Wolves as a youngster from his native Scotland and for a long time was captain of Wolves' reserve side. Taylor had transferred from Luton Town for a large fee following Jesse Pye's departure from Wolves to Luton.

Wolves' next trip was to Highbury to face Champions Arsenal, where they hadn't won for twenty-one years. The good news was that the Gunners were languishing at the foot of the table after only managing 1 point from their first five games.

---

**Wolves:** Sims; Short, Pritchard; W.J. Slater, Shorthouse, Wright; Hancocks, Broadbent, Swinbourne, Wilshaw, Mullen

**Sunderland:** Cowan; Hedley, Hudgell; Anderson, Daniel, Wright (A); Bingham, Kirtley, Wright (T), Shackleton, McSeveney

# ARSENAL *v.* WOLVES

**Football League Division One at Highbury**

**Date:** Saturday 5 September 1953          **Attendance:** 60,460

---

Highbury was another of those places where Wolves had a poor record, particularly of late. The previous year, the Gunners had handed out a 5-2 thumping. The good news for Wolves' fans was that Bert Williams was to return in goal for Wolves after having missed the first five fixtures.

Wolves were inspirational, although for a long time the outcome of the game was in the balance and might have gone either way. Arsenal were going through a prolonged spell of indifferent form, but seemed to be pumped up for this game. However, it was the visitors that turned on the style in the capital, scoring three goals again to make it three in each of the last three games. Wolves laid down a bombardment so intense that it was worthy of being called a blitzkrieg, deservedly taking the lead in the 22nd minute when Peter Broadbent got his first of the season, showing all his skill and composure on the ball before slotting it past Jack Kelsey in the Gunners' goal. Unfortunately, Wolves' happiness proved to be only temporary, as 3 minutes later outside right Don Roper found the space to grab the equaliser.

Never mind – Arsenal hadn't managed more than one goal in any of their matches to date, and now they had to return to their best defensive form to keep hungry Wolves at bay. Goal-line clearances and great saves abounded, particularly those from worthy efforts by Wilshaw, Broadbent, Mullen and Hancocks, but still it was 1-1. The pace and passion showed by both sets of players was at times breathtaking, but it was Wolves that were getting the upper hand. Just past the half-hour, Jimmy Mullen sent in a low cross, and Dennis Wilshaw dived bravely to head the ball home to restore Wolves' lead. Wanderers now pressed hard for a third goal, but back again came Arsenal, and against the run of play, centre forward Cliff Holton brought Arsenal level for the second time in the match in the 41st minute; a great time to score. The teams went in for a break at 2-2.

The second half started exactly as the first half had finished, with Wolves hammering shots at the Arsenal goal. At the back, Slater and Wright were tackling fiercely and, together with Broadbent and Wilshaw, winning the midfield battle in some style, sending wingers Hancocks and Mullen away to whip over a stream of dangerous crosses; both were in devastating form. Sadly, Kelsey was up to the task, keeping out a number of goalbound efforts with a display of top-class goalkeeping. But it wasn't all one-way traffic; Bert Williams had to bring off a couple of acrobatic saves himself as the Gunners' counter-attacked whenever Wolves allowed them to.

The result was looking like a draw when Johnny Hancocks scored a goal that was as spectacular as one might ever wish to see. Again, it was Jimmy Mullen who set up the chance. There were only 2 minutes to go when his hard low cross eluded all of the Arsenal defenders, and there was

---

**Wolves 3**                               **Arsenal 2**

*Broadbent (22)*                            *Roper (25)*

*Wilshaw (31)*                              *Holton (41)*

*Hancocks (88)*

Action from Arsenal *v.* Wolves. Bert Williams catches the ball under pressure from Doug Lishman of Arsenal.

Hancocks, racing in at the far post to score with a sensational flying header; the little winger didn't get many with his head, and this was one that the best headers in the League would have been proud of. That proved to be the straw that broke the back of the Arsenal players, who suddenly seemed to know they were beaten, their heads dropped; too late for a recovery. The referee's whistle signalled a fabulous victory for Wolves. The huge 60,460 crowd had been privileged to witness a pulsating game. Mind you, most of them went home in a bad mood.

Albion ran out worthy victors at The Hawthorns, comfortably beating Tottenham 3-0, with goals from Allen and Nicholls plus an own goal by Alf Ramsey. However, their next game wouldn't be until two days after Wolves had played Liverpool; a chance to move closer to them in the table.

---

**Arsenal:** Kelsey; Wade, Evans; Forbes, Dodgin, Bowen; Roper, Logie, Holton, Lishman, Marden
**Wolves:** Williams; Short, Pritchard; W.J. Slater, Shorthouse, Wright; Hancocks, Broadbent, Swinbourne, Wilshaw, Mullen

# WOLVES V. LIVERPOOL

Football League Division One at Molineux

**Date:** Monday 7 September 1953          **Attendance:** 35,701

---

The 6 p.m. kick-off didn't adversely affect the size of the gate, the fans anticipating a victory. Wolves had a good record against the Reds; the 3-0 win in the corresponding fixture last season rightly giving the Molineux faithful hope for this game. Liverpool made four changes to their side after losing their previous game 5-1 to Preston; Wanderers were unchanged. This time Wolves didn't get three, but still won this gruelling encounter, this time with a dogged display brim-full of character.

This was one of those sleeves-up-and-get-stuck-in kind of games when the bravery and determination of certain players was there for all to see. Wolves had eleven heroes on the park, none more so than right-back John Short, who was badly injured in the 23rd minute. The referee came in for some criticism after allowing play to carry on for a long time, ignoring Short's prone figure that was obviously in need of some attention. Eventually Mr Collinge blew his whistle and beckoned on the trainer to provide treatment. Short had to leave the field for further treatment in the dressing room to a torn muscle, emerging after some time to occupy the right wing.

The second half kicked off without him, but against all advice, he insisted on returning to the field to limp along at centre forward as nuisance value if nothing else. Despite effectively losing Short for much of the 90 minutes, Wolves took the game to Liverpool, attacking at every opportunity. They got the reward their bravery deserved a minute or so before the interval through Roy Swinbourne, who rose beautifully to head home Hancocks' inch-perfect centre. After the break, Wolves continued where they left off, Billy Wright, now at right-back, playing a blinder. Then Short almost scored with a header, before Liverpool began to pile on the pressure.

Eventually something had to give, and it did, almost breaking Wolves' hearts at the same time. In the dying minutes of this drab game, the temperature suddenly shot up. With a mere 3 minutes to go, centre forward Bimpson sent a long ball down the right for Brian Jackson to chase. With almost no back-lift, the right-winger hit a sizzling shot on the run to grab a welcome equaliser for the Reds.

This late in the game, one might have thought that both teams would have settled for a draw, rather than attack and thereby risk exposing their defence by leaving a bit of a gap at the back. Not Wolves, for now they pushed hard for the winner. They kicked off. With almost every Wolves outfield player piling into the Liverpool penalty area, ironically the ball came to John Short, who was intent on capitalising upon the home defence's slowness to get back to mark their opponents. His shrewd 88th-minute pass down the middle reached the onrushing Peter Broadbent who, despite almost colliding with Roy Swinbourne, whom he appeared to brush aside, managed to keep his feet

---

**Wolves 2**
*Swinbourne (43)*
*Broadbent (88)*

**Liverpool 1**
*Jackson (87)*

Wolves' stadium, Molineux.

to slot the ball past Crossley in the Liverpool goal. Those of the crowd who hadn't left went wild; the Reds with disappointment and the Gold and Blacks with delight.

Wolves' hard-fought victory in this bruising encounter closed the gap on Albion to 1 point. However, a lot of our players suffered knocks, Short's being the worst, but the whack that Broadbent had taken was the most worrying – we didn't want to lose him at this stage of the season.

Albion played on Wednesday, their 2-2 home draw with Newcastle restoring their 2-point advantage. This time the goals came from Paddy Ryan and Ray Barlow.

---

**Wolves:** Williams; Short, Pritchard; W.J. Slater, Shorthouse, Wright; Hancocks, Broadbent, Swinbourne, Wilshaw, Mullen

**Liverpool:** Crossley; Lambert, Spicer; Saunders, Hughes, Maloney; Jackson, Liddell, Bimpson, Jones, A'Court

# WOLVES V. PORTSMOUTH

**Football League Division One at Molineux**

**Date:** Saturday 12 September 1953          **Attendance:** 36,524

---

Wolves had beaten Pompey 4-1 the previous season, but could they do it again? For this one they were forced to make a few changes to their line-up, and what a game it was. End-to-end stuff, played in a cup-tie atmosphere in front of 36,524 delighted fans. Dennis Wilshaw grabbed his first hat-trick of the season; his second for Wolves. His first had come on his memorable debut in March 1949, Swinbourne scoring the other in a game that had everything, including the kind of fantastic finish Wolves' fans had come to expect.

Wednesbury-born National Serviceman Norman Deeley came in at right half (by the way, I sat in his old desk at Holyhead Road School, Wednesbury – he'd carved his name into the underside of the lid, which is how I know), in place of Bill Slater, who would be leading the England Amateur team against Ireland in Coleraine. Len Gibbons took over at right-back in place of the still injured John Short.

In the opening few minutes it seemed quite obvious even to the most impartial in the crowd that Wolves were going to steamroller Pompey to a heavy defeat; funny how things turn out sometimes, isn't it? Dennis Wilshaw scored twice in 3 minutes to give notice that he was coming into a rich vein of form. His first, before the game was a minute old, came from a good run and cross by Johnny Hancocks. His second, 2 minutes later, was provided courtesy of a defence-splitting through ball from Billy Wright from which Wilshaw gave Platt no chance. Unfortunately, Portsmouth hadn't been given the same script and, once they had recovered from the shock of Wilshaw's early strikes, decided to have a go. Inside forward Gordon gave the visitors some measure of hope in the 7th minute, when he rounded off a neatly executed move, his shot deflecting past Williams off Shorthouse's head. Blimey! Three goals already and the game only 7 minutes old – a goal-fest was definitely on the cards.

Wolves came back at Portsmouth with a third goal from Wilshaw to complete his hat-trick. Hancocks sent over a dangerous cross that the Wolves' number ten met perfectly with his head. However, cheers turned to fears and maybe a few tears when right-winger Harris grabbed a second for Pompey; 3-2 at half-time – not a game for the faint-hearted. Portsmouth came out for the second half with all guns blazing, Gordon getting his second 3 minutes after the restart with a stunning drive from the edge of the penalty area following Harris' centre to bring the scores level at 3-3; now we were in a real scrap for the right to be called the winner.

There were a number of occasions when both teams expected to grab the winner, but somehow the two defences managed to keep the ball out of their net. In the 86th minute it looked all over for Wolves as Pompey centre forward Vaughan burst clear of Shorthouse and Wright; a goal looked

---

**Wolves 4**

*Wilshaw 3 (1, 3 and 38)*

*Swinbourne (87)*

**Portsmouth 3**

*Gordon 2 (7 and 48)*

*Harris (44)*

inevitable until Bert Williams charged out of his goal to whip the ball away from the big number nine's foot as he was about to shoot. Then with 3 minutes remaining on the clock in what was an almost last-ditch attack, Roy Swinbourne snatched victory from the jaws of a draw. Right half Pickett was pressurised into making a hasty back pass, which eluded Platt as the goalkeeper vainly stretched for the ball, and there was Swinbourne following up to slot the ball into an empty net to huge cheers from the Wolves fans.

In the dying seconds of the game, Platt kept the score at 4-3 with a fabulous diving save from a Hancocks thunderbolt, and then he combined with Reid to just about manage to scrape the ball away from his goal line. A couple of seconds later the referee blew for time and the Wolves' fans breathed a huge sigh of relief at the end of another nail-biting finish; 4-3 to Wolves. Talk about Wolves giving their fans a bad case of the collywobbles! Wolves should have literally run away with this seven-goal thriller, Swinbourne missing a number of half chances, and Wolves certainly missed the searching balls from Bill Slater. Actually, we needn't have worried, because in the end Wolves stitched up Pompey like a kipper and hung them out to dry, and that's no lie!

Now Wolves were beginning to look really good, playing with determination and fire; five wins from their last five games. On the other side of the Black Country, Albion were also on a roll, unbeaten in their first eight games. A magnificent 4-1 victory over Burnley at Turf Moor, courtesy of two goals from Nicholls plus one each from Allen and Ryan, did the trick.

The top of the table now looked good for the West Midlands, with Villa moving into fourth spot behind Huddersfield. The top two were those boys from the Black Country:

|  | PLD | W | D | L | F | A | PTS |
|---|---|---|---|---|---|---|---|
| Albion | 8 | 6 | 2 | 0 | 19 | 5 | 14 |
| **Wolves** | **8** | **6** | **0** | **2** | **22** | **15** | **12** |

**Wolves:** Williams; Gibbons, Pritchard; Deeley, Shorthouse, Wright; Hancocks, Broadbent, Swinbourne, Wilshaw, Mullen

**Portsmouth:** Platt; Gunter, Mansell; Pickett, Reid, Dickinson; Harris, Gordon, Vaughan, Mundy, Henderson

# LIVERPOOL v. WOLVES

**Football League Division One at Anfield**

**Date:** Wednesday 16 September 1953                    **Attendance:** 29,848

Wolves' first draw of the season came at Anfield, in yet another close encounter. Every winning run has to end sometime, and I suppose it was really too much to expect that Wanderers would extend their run of five wins out of five, especially as it was away to Liverpool, a physically strong side. Wolves' players' legs would certainly testify to this fact following the recent win over today's opponents at Molineux, and who held the proud record of forty-nine years in the First Division.

The Reds had beaten Wolves 2-1 at Anfield in the previous season. However, they had lost the last five games before this one, including the defeat by Wolves, and so were desperate to halt their slide down the table, which had taken them to third from bottom. The injury to John Short hadn't cleared up and so Cullis had to shuffle his defence, moving Billy Wright to right-back, with Bill Slater returning to action at left half in his place, and young Norman Deeley retaining the number four shirt. Liverpool fielded the same team that had played at Molineux. Wolves opened up well, looking dangerous and likely to score with each attack; however, it took them until 5 minutes before the break to gain the lead. Again, it was Dennis Wilshaw who was on target to score his ninth of the season, in his ninth start.

A hopeful through-ball bounced off a Liverpool defender, and Wilshaw made sure he was first to the ball. He quickly brought it under control and cleverly beat two men to shoot past Crossley; a wonderful individual goal.

Wolves started the second half as they had finished the first, on the attack. The main fault was that the forwards seemed to want to walk the ball in; one touch or one pass too many was the problem. Johnny Hancocks obviously decided to change things and opted for a much more direct method; Crossley's hands must have hurt as he beat out his fierce drive. A few minutes later, the diminutive winger sent in another vicious shot that again cannoned off the Liverpool 'keeper's hands. Then, on 58 minutes, Wolves were denied a good goal by referee Collinge. Mullen's centre eluded Crossley and Swinbourne who fell on the goal line. Hancocks was first to the ball to prod it home with delight, only to turn in disgust as the referee disallowed the goal because he felt that Swinbourne was in an offside position!

Just after the hour, centre forward Bimpson hit Wolves' bar with a fierce cross-shot and then, in the 69th minute and pretty much against the run of play, Liverpool sent the 29,848 crowd wild. Jackson's deep centre was headed back across the area by A'Court, the ball bounced dangerously around Wolves' goalmouth, eluding all attempts at a clearance by Wolves' defence. Emerging from the mêlée, suddenly there was inside left Bill Jones to scramble home the equaliser.

This 1-1 draw was a powerful game in every sense of the word. Wolves didn't have it all their own way by any means; Billy Liddell and Bill Jones looked dangerous and, with Alan A'Court making some

---

**Liverpool 1**

*Jones (69)*

**Wolves 1**

*Wilshaw (40)*

# LIVERPOOL v. WOLVES

Alan A'Court of Liverpool.

penetrating runs down the left wing, Wolves had often been forced to defend in numbers. Bert Williams had to be alert a couple of times to prevent a goal. Billy Wright, playing in an unaccustomed role, did well to keep a hold on A'Court, with Bill Shorthouse just about managing to rein in Bimpson and Liddell, and with Pritchard having another solid game at left-back. Slater and Deeley were everywhere, the youngster giving a tireless performance supporting his attack and defence whenever required. Both half-backs frequently halted the Liverpool forwards with some excellent tackling.

In the end Wolves probably did enough to have won the game. Still, the fans couldn't complain too much; after all, 1 point is better than none, isn't it? Those that watched this game were treated to an evening of English football at its best; no quarter given and none asked for. When the final reckoning came at the end of the season, Liverpool found themselves at the bottom of the League and were relegated to the Second Division. The day after the game, young Norman Deeley had to return to Germany to link up with his army unit; his fourteen days' leave allowed him to play in two First Division games.

Now things were beginning to hot up in the title race; Nicholls grabbed his first hat-trick of the campaign as Albion murdered Newcastle 7-3 at St James' Park to continue their unbeaten start. The other scorers were Allen (2), Griffin and Ryan. This was the Baggies' seventh win of the season in nine games, the other two being drawn. They sat proudly at the top of the League on 16 points, 3 ahead of Wolves.

Wolves announced that they were pleased to return to the 'bob' gate, i.e. 1s, on the North and South Bank terraces for the forthcoming historic first floodlit game at Molineux on 30 September. Other prices were: Waterloo Road Stand centre 4s 3d, wings 3s 6d, Molineux Street Stand 3s 6d and 1s 9d in the enclosures.

---

**Liverpool:** Crossley; Lambert, Spicer; Saunders, Hughes, Maloney; Jackson, Liddell, Bimpson, Jones, A'Court
**Wolves:** Williams; Wright, Pritchard; Deeley, Shorthouse, W.J. Slater; Hancocks, Broadbent, Swinbourne, Wilshaw, Mullen

# BLACKPOOL v. WOLVES

**Football League Division One at Bloomfield Road**

**Date:** Saturday 19 September 1953          **Attendance:** 35,074

---

Directly after the Liverpool match, Stan Cullis took his team to Blackpool for a spot of bracing sea air, and to keep his players completely focused on the task in hand a few days later. Facing up to the 1953 FA Cup winners at Bloomfield Road was a daunting task for most teams. Wolves hadn't won there since 1949, and had lost 2-0 the season before. This season might be no different, as Blackpool had already won three out of their four home games.

The largest Bloomfield Road crowd of the season to date, 35,074, turned out to watch this game. The double dose of bad news for Wolves was that the legendary 'Wizard of the Dribble', Stanley Matthews, who had missed Blackpool's last two games with a groin strain, would make the starting line-up, and that at centre forward for the seasiders would be England's Stan Mortensen, hat-trick hero of the Cup final. In fact, apart from Kelly for Robinson at left half, this was the team that had won the Cup.

Jack Short was still injured, so once again Billy Wright was asked to play at right-back. Cullis was also forced into a couple of additional and unwelcome changes to his line-up: Norman Deeley, who was still doing his National Service, wasn't available, and so Ray Chatham was drafted in to replace him. Bill Slater had again been selected to play for the England Amateur side, ironically against South Africa at Selhurst Park, and was therefore also unavailable to face his former club. Bill Baxter deputised.

It was amazing that with two such attack-minded teams this match should end 0-0. Wolves' game plan was both simple and effective, and it almost worked. Close-marking and quick tackling allied to fast attacking meant that they might have scored from any number of early attacks had not Blackpool goalkeeper George Farm proved equal to everything Wolves threw at him. Having said this, Jackie Mudie should have scored for the home side on a couple of occasions, but wasted the opportunities that came his way.

The seasiders' all-star attack was made to look fairly ordinary, as Bill Shorthouse kept England ace Stan Mortensen quiet all afternoon. Chatham and Baxter also did well in their first appearance of the season, with Billy Wright again outstanding, this time against one of the fastest left-wingers in the League, Bill Perry, scorer of the winning goal in the previous season's FA Cup final. In fact, the whole of Wolves' defence was as solid as a rock; and I'm not talking about Blackpool Rock either!

Wolves' fears were raised when Dennis Wilshaw was crocked when he took a bad knock on his thigh a few minutes before the interval, resulting in him limping through the rest of the match.

Four fantastic wingers were on view. For the home side there was Perry and the inspirational Matthews, who had been well marshalled throughout this match by Bill Baxter and Roy Pritchard,

---

Blackpool 0                                        Wolves 0

Stan Mortensen, Blackpool.

and for Wolves there was the excellent Johnny Hancocks and Jimmy Mullen. The latter two gave Blackpool's full-backs a torrid time in this hard-fought and well-earned result, particularly Mullen, who gave Blackpool right-back Shimwell the runaround all afternoon.

At The Hawthorns, Albion slipped up, losing for the first time in ten starts. Goals from Barlow and Griffin weren't enough to prevent Charlton Athletic running out 3-2 winners. Unfortunately, by drawing at Blackpool, Wolves failed to capitalise upon the Baggies' ill fortune and thereby close the gap still further; however there were now only 2 points separating the Black Country rivals. The Baggies had 16 points, Wolves 14.

Everyone was talking about the forthcoming first game under Wolves' brand new floodlights. Work had progressed well and all was expected to be ready for the inaugural match against the South African tourists at the end of the month. Back at Molineux and unbeaten in seven games, Wolves next met rising stars Chelsea, while Albion faced Sheffield Wednesday at Hillsborough.

---

**Blackpool:** Farm; Shimwell, Garrett; Fenton, Johnston, Kelly; Matthews, Taylor, Mortensen, Mudie, Perry

**Wolves:** Williams; Wright, Pritchard; Chatham, Shorthouse, Baxter; Hancocks, Broadbent, Swinbourne, Wilshaw, Mullen

# WOLVES V. CHELSEA

Football League Division One at Molineux

**Date:** Saturday 26 September 1953          **Attendance:** 36,134

Wolves' fans prayed that ace sharpshooter Dennis Wilshaw would make a quick recovery from his knock, and so continue his deadly partnership with Mullen on Wolves' left. The good news was that he had, and so Wolves were back to full strength for the first time in four games. Jack Short had also recovered from injury, and with Slater and Wright back in their usual positions, Wolves' fans anticipated a good performance, building on their unbeaten run and last year's 2-2 draw.

What they got was miles better. In fact, it was a rout! A rampant Wolves walloped Chelsea 8-1 to equal their best victory since defeating Grimsby by the same score in August 1947. A hat-trick for star of the show Johnny Hancocks, a brace for Roy Swinbourne, plus goals from Peter Broadbent, Jimmy Mullen and Dennis Wilshaw did the damage. But really, this was the Hancocks and Mullen show, with Wolves' dynamic duo in irrepressible form, tormenting and taunting the Chelsea defenders with a dazzling 90-minute display straight out of the top draw.

The fun started as early as the 3rd minute, when centre half Ron Greenwood gave away a stupid and needless penalty by unnecessarily handling a cross from Jimmy Mullen. Johnny Hancocks proved that he was still an ace penalty-taker by crashing the ball home to put Wolves one up. The game ebbed and flowed for a while, with chances coming at both ends, although to be fair, most fell to Wolves. It was lucky for the Blues that goalkeeper Robertson was in fine form, as he almost single-handedly denied Wolves the second goal that their excellent approach play deserved. Then just after the half-hour, a Chelsea defender made a hash of a clearance, the ball landing at the feet of Wolves' right-winger with Robertson out of his goal. In an instant, Hancocks brought the ball under control before smashing a low shot wide of the goalkeeper and into the Pensioners' net from 35 yards out. It was 2-0 at the break, with Wolves already looking unstoppable.

A few cups of blood later, Wolves' forwards got back to the job in hand, scoring six in the second half. First, Hancocks and Mullen swapped a few trademark passes before setting up Dennis Wilshaw for his almost customary goal 3 minutes after the restart; a fine header that beat Robertson all ends up to make it three. Another wonderful crossfield ball from Mullen, and Hancocks delighted the faithful with his third goal of this game in the 54th minute; a hat-trick was nothing less than the winger deserved. Next, it was Roy Swinbourne's turn to get in on the goal-scoring action, the big number nine blasting home a superb volley from close range from Slater's inch-perfect pass – 5-0! Wow! The visitors weren't actually being overrun – they were playing some good stuff – however, Wolves were simply irresistible.

---

**Wolves 8**

*Hancocks 3 (penalty 3, 31 and 54)*
*Wilshaw (48), Swinbourne 2 (61 and 79)*
*Broadbent (71), Mullen (86)*

**Chelsea 1**

*Bentley (penalty) (76)*

Roy Bentley, Chelsea.

Now it was Peter Broadbent's turn to score, and a fine goal it was too, nipping in between two defenders to flick the ball past Robertson in the 71st minute. Not long after this there was another goal; however this time it wasn't a Wolves' player who scored. Chelsea were awarded a penalty, and up stepped England centre forward Roy Bentley to belt the ball towards Wolves' goal. But there was the 'Cat', in fine form, leaping to parry the ball, a great save from Williams. Unfortunately, the ball rebounded to Bentley as he followed up his spot kick, and he calmly slotted a consolation goal for the Londoners before Bert could recover. Chelsea must have thought they had weathered the storm, but Wolves were by no means done yet.

The only Wolves' forward who hadn't got his name on the scoreboard at this time was Jimmy Mullen, and he rectified this omission in the 86th minute by rounding off an excellent move with a great header. This was shortly after Swinbourne had got his second of the afternoon in the 79th minute. And that, as they say, was that.

Chelsea had lost Smith and Greenwood for short periods during the second half through injury, and maybe this had a bearing on the number of goals scored; Wolves' fans didn't believe so. This was a fabulous 8-1 victory over a good side that was playing well, a delightful romp from start to finish, and one that confirmed Wolves' status as a top team – one of the elite of the First Division.

---

**Wolves:** Williams; Short, Pritchard; W.J. Slater, Shorthouse, Wright; Hancocks, Broadbent, Swinbourne, Wilshaw, Mullen

**Chelsea:** Robertson; Sillett, Willemse; Armstrong, Greenwood, Saunders; , Smith (J), Lewis, Bentley McNichol, Blunstone

# WOLVES v. SOUTH AFRICA

## Floodlit Friendly at Molineux

**Date:** Wednesday 30 September 1953          **Attendance:** 33,681

---

On the same day, Griffin, Nicholls and Lewere on target as Albion beat the Owls 3-2 at Hillsborough to stay 2 points ahead of Wolves in the title race. However, this monumental 8-1 victory certainly improved Wolves' goal average considerably. Both teams had played 11 games and had scored 31 goals; West Brom had conceded only 13, 4 less than Wolves.

The next game at Molineux was the first played under Wolves' new floodlights; however, Wanderers were slightly beaten to the punch, as it were. Brierley Hill staged their first ever floodlit match at their Cottage Street ground on Monday 28 September, against local rivals Lye Town. The cost of their system was in excess of £1,000, and consisted of four steel towers, each bearing 9 x 1,500 watt floodlights. Some years later, I played centre forward in a game there: I could hardly see a flippin' thing!

Wolves had successfully toured South Africa during May and June 1951, playing and winning all 12 matches, scoring 60 goals, conceding only 5, and in the process winning many friends and admirers. Now Wolves were to repay that genuine hospitality by entertaining the South African tourists at Molineux. Wanderers' opponents had done well on their English tour to date, drawing 2-2 against Arsenal under the Highbury lights a week earlier. Before that, they had beaten an England amateur side that included Wolves' Bill Slater 4-0 at Selhurst Park, Charlton Athletic 3-1, British Universities 3-1, and Norfolk FA 4-2, and had also drawn 2-2 with Birmingham County FA. Obviously, they were no pushovers.

Before moving on to the details of this historic match, a word about Wolves' first floodlighting system. Wanderers' board decided that they wanted to see Molineux equipped with the brightest, most up-to-date floodlighting system that money could buy. After all, the club was among the most successful in the country, and therefore could afford the best. The contract was awarded to France's Electric Ltd of Darlaston. The firm's Managing Director, Mr W.G. France, applied his mind to solving the not-insignificant problems involved. He enhanced his knowledge with valuable information of this infant technology from the continent and America.

The story goes that he built a scale model of the Molineux pitch, complete with model floodlight towers, on the dining table of his Bilston home. Mr France calculated that the towers holding the floodlights would have to be high enough to ensure that glare would be almost negligible for both players and spectators. His meticulous research included such diverse things as checking the probable maximum height that a ball could be kicked, and the effect of reflection from blades of grass made shiny by rain or dew. When it was finished, the system was reported to have cost around £10,000 and involved 270 tons of concrete, nearly 20 tons of

---

**Wolves 3**                              **South Africa 1**
  *Mullen (32)*                                *Gibson (48)*
  *Broadbent (34)*
  *Swinbourne (86)*

Wolves' legendary winger
Johnny Hancocks.

steelwork, plus 6,000 yards of electrical wiring, all controlled from a nine-inch by three-inch push-button switch panel. The four steel towers were erected by Wilfred Robbins Ltd of Great Bridge, each comprising four sets of fifteen lights: 12 x 1,500 watt lamps, plus 3 x 1,000 watt projectors, which illuminated the goalmouth at the far ends of the field, each tower having provision for additional lights. Back-up was provided via a diesel generator, which also provided emergency lighting for stands, passageways, bars and offices. The system was a fantastic feat of electrical and structural engineering, and reportedly cost a mere 7s 6d an hour to run!

The honour of playing the very first floodlit game at Molineux introduced a measure of controversy. This privilege had been promised to Glasgow Celtic, with the match originally scheduled to be played on Wednesday 14 October 1953. However, as the system was ready for use well before that date, it seemed a pity not to use it. There was already a game against South Africa organised for 30 September. Wolves' board weighed all of the factors. The inaugural floodlit match should be as grand an affair as was possible, and there was little merit in an unnecessary delay. The match against the South Africa tourists definitely fitted all of the criteria, and so after much deliberation this game was chosen for that honour. The game was scheduled to take place on the afternoon of 30 September – now this was switched from what might have been a dull Wednesday afternoon fixture into something that would live in the memory of all who witnessed it. Probably only a gate of between 5,000 and 6,000 would have been at the afternoon match, as most people would be working. Allying the first use of the new floodlights to an international match would be something to see. This new thinking on the staging of this truly semi-social occasion was now made

# WOLVES V. SOUTH AFRICA

possible by the generosity of the Celtic board, whose directors readily agreed to withdraw when the situation was explained to them – and so the stage was set for what was to be the start of Wolves' journey into floodlight legend when, 'out of darkness, came floodlights'.

This first of many games under the brand new Molineux floodlights was a truly magical occasion, one that was christened by the press as 'Football in Wonderland' and 'Football in Fairyland', among many other descriptions. Over 33,000 good-humoured and somewhat curious fans turned out for the 7.45 p.m. kick-off, undaunted by the threat of rain, which in any case cleared up well before the match was due to start. The directors were probably a little disappointed that the gate wasn't bigger for this monumentally important occasion.

South African-born Eddie Stuart led Wolves out on the night, watched from the stand by Wolves' usual team captain Bill Shorthouse, who had stepped down to allow Stuart the honour of captaining Wolves against his native country. Wolves were resplendent in their new luminous gold shirts, which contrasted sharply with the bright green shirts of the South Africans.

The match kicked off to enthusiastic applause and developed into a showcase for Wolves' power play, when good football, matched with excellent sportsmanship was displayed in abundance.

The visitors played well but couldn't match Wolves' quicker thinking and movement, although their individual speed surprised a lot of people, as did their outstanding ball control, particularly that of their two inside forwards, Warren and Gibson. Goalkeeper Rudham, who had played against Wolves on their 1951 South African tour, had a magnificent game. He had already been besieged with offers from several English Football League clubs, but like the rest of his colleagues, he was under a two-year non-professional embargo. Twenty-year-old centre forward Salton was also attracting lots of interest after scoring five goals in the tourists' first two games. That night, Wolves' dynamic wingers Johnny Hancocks and Jimmy Mullen were in tremendous form. Together with wing-halves Bill Slater and Billy Wright, they gave a fabulous exhibition of long crossfield passing.

Wolves ran out comfortable 3-1 winners and, with a little more luck, might have scored more than three. Jimmy Mullen got Wolves' first on 32 minutes, then 2 minutes later Peter Broadbent lashed in a terrific narrow-angle cross-shot to put Wolves 2 up at half-time. Three minutes after the restart, Gibson headed a goal for South Africa to bring the visitors a measure of hope, but it was not to be their day. Four minutes from time Roy Swinbourne deflected a Hancocks cross past the impressive Rudham to wrap it up for Wolves at 3-1.

The two teams had provided the crowd with an enjoyable evening of first-class football, an experience that the South Africans said they'd never forget. To Wolverhampton's credit, the biggest crowd to watch the tourists on their tour had turned out to see them despite the fact that the weather was a bit dodgy. There weren't many people who saw this one that would want to miss the next floodlit match at Molineux, against Celtic.

As a memento of their visit, the South African players and officials were presented with a Walsall-made leather wallet and a Brierley Hill-made cut-glass bowl, all of the players being amateurs and therefore not eligible to be paid. The president of the South African FA said that Wolves had made a big impression in his country in 1951, and had reaffirmed this on this visit to Wolverhampton. It had been a great night for Wolves fans, a taster for the wonderful floodlit football matches that were to follow; football at Molineux would never be the same again.

FLOODLIGHT MATCH

**Wolverhampton Wanderers**

*v.*

**SOUTH AFRICA**

*at*

**MOLINEUX GROUNDS**
WOLVERHAMPTON

*WEDNESDAY, SEPTEMBER 30th, 1953*
Kick-off 7-45 p.m.

**3d.** *Official Programme* **3d.**

Front cover of the programme for Wolves *v*. South Africa, the inaugural floodlit match at Molineux.

To keep the night games as something special, the Wolves board planned only four or five floodlit games per year. Despite that announcement, the next match was already planned for one month's time, when Glasgow Celtic would be Wolves' opponents. Right now Wolves were off to Sheffield to play United in the League. The Baggies would be at home to Middlesbrough.

---

**Wolves:** Williams; Short, Pritchard; W.J. Slater, Stuart, Wright, Hancocks, Broadbent, Swinbourne, Stockin, Mullen. (At that time, Bill Slater held amateur status)

**South Africa:** Rudham; Machanik, Jacobson; Dow, Naish, Jacques; Claassens, Warren, Salton, Gibson, Le Roux

# SHEFFIELD UNITED v. WOLVES

**Fooball League Division One at Bramhall Lane**

**Date:** Saturday 3 October 1953 **Attendance:** 36,303

At Bramall Lane, Wolves faced a newly promoted Sheffield United team in determined mood; they didn't want to lose the momentum of their best start since 1951/52. This was a battle royal indeed, a thrilling game of all-out attacking football, with Wolves twice coming from behind to earn a magnificent draw.

Wanderers' full-strength side started magnificently and, imbued by their eight-game unbeaten run in the League that had taken them into second place only 2 points behind leaders Albion, they attacked at will. Hancocks and Mullen were once again in a rampant mood. In the first 10 minutes of the game, both sent over a rich stream of crosses that could, and should, have resulted in a goal, the best being a Broadbent header that slammed against the Blades' crossbar following a scintillating combination of crossfield passing from Hancocks and Mullen. This was cultured football at its very best, and played at a breathtaking pace.

With the 10-minute mark approaching, Johnny Hancocks eventually opened Wolves' account with a well-taken goal. Surely, the floodgates would open once again. In fact, the opposite happened. The Blades made a switch, Jimmy Hagan drifting away from the inside right position, where he was being dominated by Billy Wright, to produce a masterful display of shrewd passing that inspired United to greater deeds. The home side reaped the benefits in the 18th minute, when a lovely goal by right-winger Alf Ringstead brought them back into the game. Suddenly, it was Sheffield on the offensive and Wolves on the back foot, as Hagan began to run the show.

United went deservedly ahead through reserve centre forward Bottom, who scored a marvellous solo goal on 25 minutes to put the wind up the Wolves. Stung into action, they now pressed forward menacingly. It was Dennis Wilshaw that came up with the equaliser, with a fine individual goal in the 31st minute; 2-2 at half-time.

The second half was a much more scrappy affair, and sadly for Wolves the Blades began to get the upper hand largely through the intelligent prompting of Hagan and Brook, and it was no surprise when in the 48th minute Ringstead scored again to give United the lead that their improved play deserved.

Wolves were having problems getting going and, at times, their defensive flanks were at sixes and sevens, despite some outstanding work by Wright and Slater. Short was looking decidedly uncomfortable against the speedy Hawksworth, and with Pritchard too often given the runaround by the trickery of Ringstead, it began to look as though their unbeaten run would come to an end. But football isn't like that. Just when things looked at their worst, a superb goal from Roy Swinbourne earned Wolves a draw with only 5 minutes of play remaining. The bustling centre

---

**Sheffield United 3**
*Ringstead 2 (18 and 48)*
*Bottom (25)*

**Wolves 3**
*Hancocks (10)*
*Wilshaw (31)*
*Swinbourne (85)*

forward burst through the heart of the Sheffield defence to draw Burgin before firing the ball into the net to bring the scores level at 3-3.

Wolves had kept their unbeaten record, but only just, in what the locals claimed was the most exciting game seen at Bramall Lane for a long time. The game was attended by the chairman of the England International Selection Committee, Harold Shentall. With the forthcoming Home International Championship and World Cup qualifier against Wales coming up in a couple of weeks' time, he was running the rule over a number of players to include in the England party. He must have been impressed by the dynamic left-wing play of Jimmy Mullen, who was in quite magnificent form, as was Johnny Hancocks on Wolves' opposite flank. Almost equally as impressive were Bill Slater and Dennis Wilshaw, and surely it wouldn't be long before Broadbent won his first cap. What was certain was that Billy Wright would again captain the England team where he had become such a permanent fixture; it was impossible to think of an England side without him.

West Brom beat Middlesbrough 2-1 to open up a 3-point gap over Wolves; Nicholls and Lee getting the goals.

A disappointing Wolves performance saw them lose 3-1 to Bury in a floodlit friendly at Gigg Lane on Monday 5 October 1953. Then it was back to League action in Geordieland against the Magpies, with Albion taking on Huddersfield Town at The Hawthorns.

Billy Wright in action.

---

**Sheffield United:** Burgin; Furniss, Shaw (G); Shaw (J), Tower, Rawson; Ringstead, Hagan, Bottom, Brook, Hawksworth

**Wolves:** Williams; Short, Pritchard; W.J. Slater, Shorthouse, Wright; Hancocks, Broadbent, Swinbourne, Wilshaw, Mullen

# NEWCASTLE UNITED v. WOLVES

**Football League Division One at St James' Park**

**Date:** Saturday 10 October 1953          **Attendance:** 39,913

---

Ho'way the lads! Wolves came away from the North-East in triumphant mood, despite being forced into playing a much depleted team due to key players being selected for international duty. It's worth noting that back in 1953 international matches were often played on the same day as League games, and the FA had first call on the players. No allowance was made regarding the importance of League fixtures; internationals got first call. All but one of Wolves' left side, Billy Wright, Dennis Wilshaw and Jimmy Mullen, were called up by England manager Walter Winterbottom for the Home International Championship/World Cup qualifying game against Wales at Ninian Park in Cardiff, the first international match of the season. Ron Flowers was drafted in at left half, Ron Stockin came in at inside left, and Les Smith took over on the left-wing.

In this fixture in the previous season, Wanderers had managed a creditable 1-1 draw, but hadn't won at St James' Park since 28 February 1903. So not many people gave this weakened Wolves' team much of a chance with three reserves in the line up.

When the home side took the lead through Tommy Mulgrew before the game had reached the 10-minute mark, it looked as though history would repeat itself. Tyneside folk hero 'Wor' Jackie Milburn was at his usual dangerous best, constantly threatening to score, and Bert Williams had to be on top form to keep the score down to 1-0 at the interval. Roy Pritchard plugged many a gap in Wolves' defence, despite suffering a painful kick to the leg. Bill Slater also took a knock, which obviously caused him some pain.

Wolves came out for the second half in much more determined fashion, taking the game to the home side. Captain Bill Shorthouse had been a tower of strength before the break, and now pushed and prompted his forwards onto the attack. Swinbourne in particular showed Wolves' old 'up-and-at-'em' style with a display of powerful and robust centre-forward play, at times causing real chaos in the centre of Newcastle's defence, where Brennan and Scoular often looked to be in a daze. Broadbent was spraying the ball around quite beautifully; surely, Wolves must get a reward for all their effort?

Eventually, the equaliser came, and deservedly so. This time it was Les Smith, normally a right-winger, playing in Mullen's left-wing berth who, in the 81st minute, scored Wolves' first with a crashing shot of Hancocks-esque power which left Ronnie Simpson in the Geordie's goal groping at thin air, as well as threatening to break the net. Now Wolves had Newcastle on the back foot, and pressed hard for the winner.

Less than 2 minutes were left on the clock when Wolves were awarded a free-kick outside the home team's penalty area. Johnny Hancocks placed the ball deliberately and paced out his run; the

---

**Newcastle United 1**
*Mulgrew (9)*

**Wolves 2**
*Smith (81)*
*Swinbourne (88)*

# Newcastle United v. Wolves

England manager Walter Winterbottom.

Newcastle defenders lined up knowing what was coming. The little winger commenced his run-up, but deceived everyone by squaring the ball to Swinbourne instead of shooting, a path to goal had opened up and Wolves' number nine placed his accurate shot into the net to move into double figures for the season, like his strike partner Dennis Wilshaw. The partisan crowd of almost 40,000 was stunned; it hadn't been the best quality football, but Wolves had won at St James' for the first time in fifty years.

At Ninian Park in Cardiff, England emphatically beat Wales 4-1 in front of 61,000 fans. Three Wolves' players played for England in this match: Billy Wright, Dennis Wilshaw and Jimmy Mullen, Wilshaw scoring twice on his England debut, with centre forward Nat Lofthouse getting the other two. All four England goals came from headers.

England: Merrick; Garrett, Eckersley; Wright (Capt.), Johnston, Dickinson; Finney, Quixall, Lofthouse, Wilshaw, Mullen.

Across the Black Country, the Baggies beat Huddersfield Town 4-0 to maintain their 3-point lead over Wolves. A Ronnie Allen hat-trick, plus one from Nicholls, did the damage.

Wolves took a quick break from the League with their second match under the Molineux floodlights.

---

**Newcastle United:** Simpson; Cowell, Batty; Scoular, Brennan, Casey; Milburn, Mulgrew, White, Keery, Mitchell

**Wolves:** Williams; Short, Pritchard; W.J. Slater, Shorthouse, Flowers; Hancocks, Broadbent, Swinbourne, Stockin, Smith

# WOLVES V. CELTIC

**Floodlit Friendly at Molineux**
**Date:** Wednesday 14 October 1953          **Attendance:** 41,820

This game kicked off at 7.30 p.m., and once again, Wolves came up trumps for the fans by beating Celtic 2-0. Manager Stan Cullis decided upon a number of changes for this game, the most notable being the debut of seventeen-year-old Tipton lad Bobby Mason. Peter Broadbent, who was on the point of finishing his National Service, had been released to play for a Services eleven at White Hart Lane on the same night, and Bobby got the vote to take his place. Returning from successful England duty for this game were Billy Wright, Jimmy Mullen and Dennis Wilshaw. Roy Pritchard and Bill Slater had picked up injuries at Newcastle, so Cullis brought in Bill Guttridge and Bill Baxter to replace them. In goal, Nigel Sims again deputised for Bert Williams.

Over 40,000 turned out on a fine night to witness a great game – even better football than we saw from the South Africans, this was some of the most exhilarating seen at Molineux since the Chelsea game. The game was billed as a friendly, but both teams gave a committed performance as if fighting for League points or cup survival – exactly how football should be played. Celtic, without their Scottish international centre half Jock Stein, thrilled the bumper crowd in the first half with a display of almost incredible speed of thought and movement. They were obviously much better than we had expected. No goals at half-time was not a true reflection of the exciting football we had witnessed in the first 45 minutes.

In the second half, it seemed that the Scots' fierce attacking impetus had finally worn itself out. However, we still had to wait a long time before Wolves scored. Dennis Wilshaw was the man who did it, topping a fine team performance with two excellent goals. His first, 4 minutes from the end, brought a strong protest from the Scots, who believed that he had used his hand to control the ball. However, their objections were waved away and the goal stood.

The Celtic players were still bemoaning the referee's decision when they unnecessarily gave away a free-kick, from which Wilshaw scored his second with a cleanly executed hook-shot that flew past the Celtic goalkeeper. The Scots had their share of chances, and in fact earlier in the game twice had the ball in Wolves' net only to see both disallowed by referee Leafe.

The knowledgeable crowd showed their appreciation of Celtic's international wing half Bobby Evans. It was he that prompted the majority of Scottish raids in an all-round display brim-full with quality.

In the final analysis, Wolves lasted the pace better than Celtic, and over the 90 minutes proved to be that bit more effective. Wolves' left-back, hard-as-nails Bill 'Chopper' Guttridge, surprisingly curbed his sometimes overly aggressive style of play to result in one of his most effective games, in the process prompting a number of dangerous moves. He was a real crowd favourite, the 'Psycho'

**Wolves 2**                                   **Glasgow Celtic 0**
*Wilshaw 2 (86 and 88)*

Bobby Mason.

of his day – the fans gave him his nickname 'Chopper' – I'll bet you can guess how he earned it! Wing half Bill Baxter also had a good game. His best effort was a flashing long-range shot that was well saved by Hunter. It crowned a good performance, along with the rest of his team mates. Young Bobby Mason, in his first trial with the senior side, did well, his enthusiasm fully deserving a goal. He almost got one, but goalkeeper Hunter made the save of the game. So in the end Wolves won. Although to be fair, no one would have complained if the match had finished as a draw.

Three days later it was back to League action, as Wolves entertained one of their biggest rivals, the Red Devils from Old Trafford.

---

**Wolves:** Sims; Short, Guttridge; Baxter, Shorthouse, Wright; Hancocks, Mason, Swinbourne, Wilshaw, Mullen
**Celtic:** Hunter; Haughney, Fallon; Evans, McIlroy, Peacock; Collins, Fernie, McPhail, Walsh, Mochan

# WOLVES V. MANCHESTER UNITED

**Football League Division One at Molineux**

**Date:** Saturday 17 October 1953          **Attendance:** 40,084

---

Roy Pritchard's injury hadn't improved, and so Bill Guttridge kept his place in the starting line-up. Apart from that, Wolves were at full strength. United's team, becoming widely known as the 'Busby Babes', was packed with international stars, and Molineux's largest crowd of the season to date came to watch them, most secretly hoping for a repeat of last season's emphatic 6-2 win.

Lips were smacking in anticipation as the game kicked-off, and immediately Wolves went on the attack, once again turning on the style with their own unique brand of powerful attacking football, in the process disposing of Manchester United very efficiently indeed. Of course, the Reds in the crowd wouldn't have agreed with this – they felt that United had been on the receiving end of too much bad luck. On the balance of play in the first 45 minutes, maybe they had something of a case, but in the end, it's them that guzz in, uz counts.

On 16 minutes, England left-back Roger Byrne needlessly handled the ball in the area to give Wolves a penalty, which Johnny Hancocks dispatched clinically past goalkeeper Ray Wood. Just before the half-hour, United were back on level terms, and a bit lucky they were.

An uncharacteristic mix up in the Wolves' defence allowed centre forward Tommy Taylor to nip in and whip the ball into the net to bring the scores level. Shaken into action, the home side renewed their efforts and went close on a number of occasions. Then United came back again.

They hit a post, watched Williams produce a couple of world-class saves, and had a penalty appeal turned down by the referee. Unlucky United? Maybe. Either way, they didn't get a second, despite some marvellous right-wing play from ex-Birmingham City forward Johnny Berry.

Billy Wright was on the receiving end of a couple of excessive challenges, each taking a little time for him to run off the pain, and there's no doubt that Wanderers' effectiveness was impaired during this time. When the Wolves' captain was operating at full power, a number of magic moments were produced, resulting in a couple of excellent efforts on goal. However, it wasn't until 5 minutes before half-time that they finally got the breakthrough. Hancocks and Mullen had already provided the crowd with some thrilling wing-to-wing passing and dangerous-looking crosses. It was to one of these that Peter Broadbent rose majestically to cleverly head Wolves back in front – 2-1 at the interval was great for Wolves.

In the second period, United pressed for the equaliser and had a lot of good possession without quite managing to pose a real threat to Williams' goal. Wolves' defence absorbed everything the Reds threw at them, and then in the 72nd minute Roy Swinbourne got the better of the previously excellent Chilton to wrap up the points for Wolves with a smartly taken goal. This was a fabulous win against the most impressive team Wolves had met in the season to date.

---

**Wolves 3**
*Hancocks (penalty) (16),*
*Broadbent (40)*
*Swinbourne (72)*

**Manchester United 1**
*Taylor (29)*

# WOLVES v. MANCHESTER UNITED

Johnny Berry, Manchester United.

Albion's 2-1 victory over the Blades at Bramall Lane was a case of anything you can do, we can do better. League leaders still, they maintained their 3-point advantage over Wolves with deadly duo Allen and Nicholls again on target.

Billy Wright and Jimmy Mullen were selected to play for England in the Wembley friendly against the Rest of Europe on Wednesday 21 October 1953 to mark the FA's 75th anniversary. A crowd of 96,000 watched a cracking game in which Wolves' flying Geordie winger scored two of England's goals in a 4-4 draw. England's other goal-scorers were Stan Mortenson and Alf Ramsey, with a last-minute penalty that saved England's blushes.

England: Merrick; Ramsey, Eckersley; Wright (Capt.), Ufton, Dickinson; Matthews, Mortenson, Lofthouse, Quixall, Mullen.

For their next game Wolves faced a difficult trip to Lancashire to play against in-form England international centre forward Nat Lofthouse's Bolton.

---

**Wolves:** Williams; Short, Guttridge; W.J. Slater, Shorthouse, Wright; Hancocks, Broadbent, Swinbourne, Wilshaw, Mullen

**Manchester United:** Wood; Foulkes, Byrne; Whitefoot, Chilton, Cockburn; Berry, Pearson, Taylor, Rowley, McShane

# BOLTON WANDERERS V. WOLVES

Football League Division One at Burnden Park

**Date:** Saturday 24 October 1953       **Attendance:** 35,001

---

Unfortunately, Billy Wright had picked up an injury playing for England against Wales, and therefore wouldn't be available for this game. Bill Baxter was once again drafted in at right-half, with Bill Slater switching to left half. Bolton would be at full strength, with England's 'Lion of Vienna', Nat Lofthouse, at centre forward, so Bert Williams knew he could expect a bit of a battering. Wolves kept their unbeaten run going with this draw against their old adversaries, those other Wanderers. Bolton were also unbeaten, so both teams had a lot to lose.

Wolves shot out of the blocks like a bat out of hell, probing the Trotter's defence for an opening, with both half-backs supporting the inside forwards to produce some beautifully controlled football. The inevitable breakthrough came in the 26th minute, when Johnny Hancocks got his name on the scoreboard with a typically fierce shot. Bolton regrouped and launched a number of dangerous looking moves of their own; a couple of which had Bert Williams once again showing off the kind of form that had previously made him the automatic choice in England's goal.

First he kept out Hassall's fierce drive, then clutched a header from the same player before diving full-length to stop a rocket from Lofthouse. This concentrated pressure on Wolves' defence ultimately took its toll when inside right Willie Moir netted the equaliser a minute before half-time, following a rather neat return pass from Lofthouse that completely wrong-footed Wolves' defence. Holden did well on the right and the chance was set up. Williams ruefully picked the ball out of his net – a bad time to concede a goal, although the score of 1-1 at half-time probably flattered Wolves. In the second half Bolton were as determined to get the winner as the visitors were not to concede it, but it was Wolves who went closest. Peter Broadbent latched on to a great through ball, which he intuitively lobbed over the Bolton 'keeper, only to watch his wonderful effort slide narrowly over the bar. Then Johnny Hancocks went down the right and whipped in a great low centre that Hanson did well to push away; unfortunately, the ball ran to a defender who cleared.

Now Bolton took control of the game, with Moir, Hassall and Lofthouse all going close, Williams continuing to deny those other Wanderers a second goal. On this showing, it was doubtful if there was a better goalkeeper in the country. Lofthouse thought he'd set up the winner when he lobbed a pass over the head of Bill Shorthouse into the penalty area. Moir ran in unchallenged to smack a hard, low shot that hit Williams' legs and bounced clear. As the game neared the end, the 'Cat' produced the save of the match, tipping a thunderbolt around the post for a corner, one of many that Bolton forced in this fiercely contested game.

Despite further good work by Hassall and his colleagues, to add to Lofthouse's powerful display, Wolves' defence held out until the final whistle. Wolves had many stars that day. Bill Shorthouse

---

**Bolton Wanderers 1**

*Moir (44)*

**Wolves 1**

*Hancocks (26)*

# BOLTON WANDERERS v. WOLVES

Billy Wright shakes hands with Ernst Ocwirk before England's international match with FIFA Rest of the World at Wembley.

played a captain's role in this bruising encounter, ably supported by Guttridge, Baxter and Slater. Broadbent was elegant, Hancocks, Swinbourne, Wilshaw and Mullen always dangerous. In fact, the entire Wolves team played their part in winning this hard-fought point at Burnden Park, where the previous year they had lost 2-1. However, the undoubted man of the match was Bert Williams, and it was to him that Wolves owed a big thank you for this point.

No let-up from the Baggies, who thumped Chelsea 5-2 at The Hawthorns, the goals coming from another hat-trick by Ronnie Allen and one each from Nicholls and Lee; now they were 4 points ahead of Wolves.

In yet another floodlit friendly, a good-sized crowd of 18,680 souls turned out on Wednesday 28 October 1953 to see Third Division (South) Coventry City beat Wolves 1-0, in the second floodlit match at Highfield Road, with a Jamieson penalty shortly after half-time. This game cost Wolves dear, with both Swinbourne and Broadbent having to be withdrawn in the second half after sustaining nasty injuries. Would they make it back for the next match?

---

**Bolton Wanderers:** Hanson; Ball, Banks (T); Wheeler, Barrass, Bell; Holden, Moir, Lofthouse, Hassall, Parry
**Wolves:** Williams; Short, Guttridge; Baxter, Shorthouse, W.J. Slater; Hancocks, Broadbent, Swinbourne, Wilshaw, Mullen

# Wolves v. Preston North End

Football League Division One at Molineux

Date: Saturday 31 October 1953          Attendance: 34,211

Preston had won the corresponding fixture of the previous season 2-0 on their way to pipping Wolves for the runners-up spot in Division One. The year before that, they had beaten Wolves 4-1, so the omens weren't good. Unfortunately, the knock that Roy Swinbourne had taken at Coventry forced Cullis to shuffle his attack, Wilshaw taking the number nine jersey, with Ronnie Stockin coming in at inside left. The good news was that both Billy Wright and Peter Broadbent had recovered from injury and were available for selection. However, as the half-back line of Baxter, Shorthouse and Slater had performed so excellently at Bolton, the manager was loath to make changes. Instead he accommodated Wright at left-back, his first time in that position, in place of Roy Pritchard who was still suffering from the injury he incurred at Newcastle. Usual reserve left-back Bill Guttridge was also still on the injured list, and anyway, the legendary Tom Finney would need a man of Wright's class to look after him. As it turned out, Finney didn't make the starting eleven for Preston. In his place was a young eighteen-year-old debutant named Les Campbell; the lad did okay.

This was the thirteenth game of Wolves' unbeaten run. That said, the outcome should have been rather less fortunate for the visitors than it turned out to be. Some people held their annual Bonfire Night party on this day, and those that did certainly will have witnessed a lot more fireworks than the Molineux faithful: the game was a damp squib. There was too much of a hint of nervousness about Wolves' play – they just couldn't seem to settle down. All too often, the forwards were guilty of indecision; holding the ball too long, and running into blind alleys when an early pass might have produced a goal.

No one played really badly; in fact, on the whole the defence mopped up everything that Preston tried, but the linesman responsible for Wolves' attacking half of the field certainly didn't help. 'It's my job to prevent too much excitement,' he seemed to be saying as he constantly raised his flag for offside, mostly against Jimmy Mullen; the guy certainly succeeded.

The 0-0 half-time scoreline was as boring as the first 45 minutes had been. There were a few flashes of Wolves' characteristic power-play as the second half suddenly ignited, or perhaps sputtered into life. It was one of these flashes that brought the goal.

The move began in classic style, with Billy Wright's excellent long pass down the left to Jimmy Mullen. He in turn swung the ball right across the full width of the pitch, over the heads of the defenders, to Johnny Hancocks, who now put over a slide-rule cross at the height of the crossbar for Dennis Wilshaw to flash home a lovely header: a typical and well-rehearsed Wolves move. Why they didn't use this tactic more often in this match was a puzzle to most doyens of the game.

---

**Wolves 1**                              **Preston North End 0**
*Wilshaw (55)*

# WOLVES v. PRESTON NORTH END

Preston put in a few useful attacks, one producing a lovely shot from Wayman that forced Short to clear the ball off his goal line. Then Williams again showed his agility with an acrobatic save to keep out Cunningham's shot. The Lilywhites' right-back had been forced to play on the left-wing after taking a knock before the interval, but he showed that he could still shoot.

Wanderers' lads closed out the game on the attack, Mattinson having to be alert to chase back to scoop away Wilshaw's shot before it could cross the line, then Thompson was helpless as Bill Slater crashed in a hard drive that smacked against a post to once again foil Wolves' efforts to get a second goal. 1-0 wasn't a bad result anyway. Perhaps the absence of Roy Swinbourne was the reason behind Wolves' apparent tentativeness. Still, Wolves had now gone 13 games without being beaten.

At last Wolves moved a little closer to the Baggies, who lost 4-1 at Blackpool, Allen scoring the goal; now Albion were only 2 in front, with 26 points to Wolves' 24.

Bill Slater had already won 16 Amateur International caps when once again he was invited to play in an England Amateur trial match for Northern Counties against Southern Counties at Blackpool on the coming Saturday. To Wolves' benefit he declined the invitation, preferring instead to help in the quest for more League points. Bill had already missed two of Wolves' games to play for England Amateurs. The problem was that, if he was chosen and the FA refused to release him, he would have to play for England. The whole situation was very unfortunate for Wolves. There was speculation that it wouldn't be too long before he surrendered his amateur status; he was certainly good enough to play for England at full international level.

---

**Wolves:** Williams; Short, Wright; Baxter, Shorthouse, W.J. Slater; Hancocks, Broadbent, Wilshaw, Stockin, Mullen

**Preston North End:** Thompson; Cunningham, Walton; Mattinson, Marston, Dunn; Campbell, Hatsell, Wayman, Baxter, Morrison

# MIDDLESBROUGH V. WOLVES

Football League Division One at Ayresome Park

**Date:** Saturday 7 November 1953　　　　　**Attendance:** 23,994

---

Bostin news – Roy Swinbourne was back. Billy Wright again turned out at left-back, and turned in an excellent performance in this battle of Ayresome Park. And a battle royal it was, one that required the very best application to the task in hand from every one of Wolves' players.

On 16 minutes Roy Swinbourne grabbed the lead for Wolves, the big Wolves' number nine catching out the Boro defenders, who didn't expect him to shoot from 25 yards. Ugolini knew little about Roy's wonderful shot until it hit the back of his net. It was a truly magnificent goal which spurred the visitors to launch attack after attack, going close on many occasions, only to have their hearts temporarily broken as Arthur Fitzsimmons brought the scores level 6 minutes later.

It took Wolves until the 43rd minute to claw back the lead with a speculative long-range lofted effort from Johnny Hancocks' left foot which deceived goalkeeper Ugolini in flight; 2-1 to Wanderers at the interval.

There was just time for the crowd to get their breath back before the frenetic action started all over again. Both teams attacked as if their lives depended upon it, and chances were squandered that might otherwise have been taken, the worst miss coming from Johnny Hancocks.

The diminutive winger got himself into a great position in the centre with the Boro defence split wide open by some great running off the ball by Swinbourne and Wilshaw. He took the ball inside the penalty area, but instead of placing the ball past the goalkeeper, he screwed his shot well wide. Slater had blunted every move that Wilf Mannion had so far tried, but now it was the home side, prompted by their ace schemer, that came up with the goods, or more accurately, the equaliser. First, it was Ken McPherson sweeping in a fine 56th-minute goal through a crowd of players from Delapenha's perfect cross. Then, 17 minutes later, Jimmy Hartnett put Boro in front for the first time in the match with a great left-foot shot.

With Boro defending stoutly, time was running out for the visitors when the ball was worked out to Mullen, and in a repeat of the previous match's move, he swung the ball across to Hancocks, who in turn centred. As happened so many times, there was Dennis Wilshaw to head his thirteenth goal of the campaign, and thus bring the scores level at 3-3 with only 4 minutes remaining: a great fight back from the visitors.

Sensing victory might still be theirs, Wolves piled on the pressure and Wilshaw almost got a second to wrap up the points for Wolves, but it was not to be. The bad news for Wolves was a late injury to Broadbent; stretching to reach the ball, he badly twisted his ankle. Everyone hoped he'd make the match with West Bromwich Albion a week later.

---

**Middlesbrough 3**

*Fitzsimmons (22)*

*McPherson (56)*

*Hartnett (73)*

**Wolves 3**

*Swinbourne (16)*

*Hancocks (43)*

*Wilshaw (86)*

Against a determined Boro a draw was probably a fair result, heaven knows both teams put in enough effort to at least earn a point. Wolves were making a practice of scoring last-gasp important goals, a tribute to their fitness.

Despite the Baggies' 2-0 home win over Sunderland with goals from Barlow and Lee, Wolves were still in a great position, second in the League 3 points behind Albion, whose turn it now was to face the power-play style of the lads from the Wolverhampton side of the Black Country, in the battle of the giants. In third place was Huddersfield, 2 points adrift of our Golden Wanderers.

Before that, England played a Home International Championship/World Cup qualifier against Northern Ireland at Goodison Park, Liverpool on Wednesday 11 November 1953. Albion's Stan Rickaby won his one and only cap in this game and Jimmy Mullen retained the left-wing berth, joining Billy Wright in the England team for a welcome 3-1 victory that qualified them for the World Cup final in Switzerland in June 1954. Aside from Merrick in goal and Matthews on the right-wing, England really didn't play well. They would have to seriously improve upon this feeble display if they were going to get anything out of the forthcoming game against the reigning Olympic Champions, Hungary. England's scorers were Hassall (2) and Lofthouse.

England: Merrick; Rickaby, Eckersley; Wright, Johnson, Dickinson; Matthews, Quixall, Lofthouse, Hassall, Mullen.

Attendance: 70,000.

On the back of this excellent result, Billy Wright announced the imminent publication of his new book, *The World's My Football Pitch*, to be released on 16 November. His first book, *Captain Of England*, published three years earlier, had been an instant success.

Bad news for Wanderers fans: Wolves would be without Bill Slater for the Albion game as he had been chosen at left half for the England Amateur team to play France at Luton. He might have escaped the trial game, but this invitation to play was more of an order. After careful consideration, the decision was that neither he nor Wolves would seek in any way to embarrass his position with the England selectors by challenging his selection. At the time Slater was employed on a short-term contract by the Physical Education Department of Birmingham University, a position he hoped would be made permanent, in which case he would turn professional, albeit on a part-time basis; the feeling in the game was that he would do this anyway.

The queue for tickets for the game against the Baggies started to form outside the Molineux ticket office at 7 a.m. on 9 November. It was the custom to sell reserved seat tickets on the Monday morning prior to the next First Division match. The problem on this particular Monday was that it didn't take long for the line of fans to swell to many hundreds, many more in fact than the number

---

**Middlesbrough:** Ugolini; Bilcliff, Hepple; Bell, Robinson, Gordon; Delapenha, Mannion, McPherson, Fitzsimmons, Hartnett

**Wolves:** Williams; Short, Wright; Baxter, Shorthouse, W.J. Slater; Hancocks, Broadbent, Swinbourne, Wilshaw, Mullen

# MIDDLESBROUGH v. WOLVES

Wolves team photograph.

of available seats. Fortunately, the club recognised this fact and confirmed that disappointed fans had at least learned of their unlucky fate by 11 a.m.

Wolves announced that Roy Pritchard would be back in the starting line-up after missing four games. The bad news was that, following a week's intensive treatment on his twisted ankle, Peter Broadbent wouldn't make it. Albion would be at full strength, with Joe Kennedy making his 150th appearance.

Wolves were having a good season: unbeaten in 14 games thus far, including 7 successive wins at home. In fact, they hadn't lost at Molineux since 3 January 1953, in the previous campaign, winning all but one of the intervening 15 home games. Mind you, West Brom were doing pretty well themselves, topping the League after a great start to their season, which had seen them notch up 6 away victories out of 7. Something had to give.

# WOLVES V. WEST BROMWICH ALBION

Football League Division One at Molineux

**Date:** Saturday 14 November 1953          **Attendance:** 56,590

---

A huge crowd of 56,590 turned out for this Black Country 'old firm' derby, destined to be the highest attendance at Molineux that season. They watched an absorbing game, with Wolves getting the upper hand on their all too elaborate rivals with a goal by Geordie winger Jimmy Mullen. Even the absence of Peter Broadbent and Bill Slater didn't diminish Wolves' performance as they closed to within 1 point of the League leaders with this welcome victory.

What a game! Loads of thrills, stacks of spills, and ultimate disappointment for the stripy lot and their fans. Kicking off at 2.30 p.m., this certainly wasn't one for the football purists, but what a fantastic result!

As had been announced, the Baggies were at full strength and had won 13 of their first 17 games, losing only twice and drawing the other 2 in their march to the top of the League. In the process, their 'terrible twins' strike force of Ronnie Allen and Johnny Nicholls had scored 13 and 16 respectively, so on paper at least, they were favourites for this one. However, Wolves held a different view, and set out to prove it.

The 'Battle of the Black Country' was billed as a contrast in styles, Albion's accurate passing game, against Wolves' more direct power-play. Under an overcast sky, the dry, firm pitch certainly facilitated a fast and furious start. After only a couple of minutes of the game, Albion's right-back Stan Rickaby should have played the ball out of defence by putting his foot through it; row Z beckoned. Instead, his hesitation allowed Johnny Hancocks to whip the ball away before sending Jimmy Mullen clear down the left.

It looked as though the Geordie intended to send over one of his trademark centres, but this time it was soon obvious that the ball was going to be too close to the goalkeeper. For some reason, the normally reliable Norman Heath in the Baggies goal misjudged the flight of the ball, probably expecting to feel a strong challenge from Roy Swinbourne, which incidentally didn't come. The ball flew straight into the West Brom net to give Wolves a 4th-minute lead, and as it turned out, the winner. Maybe it was a shot after all. Heath looked embarrassed as he picked the ball out of his net and punted it upfield with some venom; his colleagues couldn't believe it.

Sleeves were rolled up even further as the Throstles adopted more of a direct style, á la Wolves. Half-time came and went, battle was renewed, and at times the crowd were treated to glimpses of Albion's trademark short-passing game, which on this day produced little, as at least one too many passes seemed to be the order of the day. Albion's players seemed to want to make five or six passes when two or three would have got the job done.

---

**Wolves 1**
*Mullen (4)*

          **West Bromich Albion 0**

# WOLVES v. WEST BROMWICH ALBION

Most of the time, Wolves' tough and well-executed tackling, sometimes ferocious in intensity and which, by the way, was often uncompromising, put an end to Albion's pretty-pattern progressions around the park. Mullen and Hancocks continued to torment Albion's full-backs Rickaby and Millard, and maybe their efforts should have produced a second goal.

Ronnie Allen actually went closest to scoring from one of Albion's more direct approaches, this one involving only three passes, luckily for Wolves. His fine lunging header from Dudley's grub-hunter of a cross was thwarted by a post, the ball bouncing into the grateful hands of Bert Williams. Then Allen instinctively met a Griffin centre, hooking in a sweet shot that looked to be going in. Not so; the 'Cat' flung his body sideways to miraculously claw the ball away to safety; brilliant stuff from Bert.

Aside from Wolves' winner, Norman Heath in Albion's goal also had his moments, keeping out goalbound efforts from Wilshaw and Mullen, who was still giving Rickaby a torrid time. Suddenly it was all over. Wolves' supporters went crackers, cheering their heroes for all they were worth as they left the field; they had beaten their closest rivals and closed the gap between them to a single point. Fantastic!

Man of the Match Billy Wright's display of boundless enthusiasm and non-stop running was Wolves' greatest source of inspiration on a day when both defences were very much in control. Joe Kennedy was outstanding for Albion and it's fair to say that Len Millard did well to keep Hancocks quiet for long periods. 1-0! The game was jam-packed full of incidents and excitement, giving both sets of fans plenty to talk about for some time.

This great victory by Wolves pegged Albion's lead at the top to 1 point.

|         | PLD | W  | D | L | F  | A  | PTS |
|---------|-----|----|---|---|----|----|-----|
| Albion  | 18  | 13 | 2 | 3 | 47 | 22 | 28  |
| **Wolves** | **18** | **11** | **5** | **2** | **45** | **26** | **27** |

Wolves' unbeaten run had now stretched to 15 games – 13 home wins in succession, 8 this season.

---

**Wolves:** Williams; Short, Pritchard; Baxter, Shorthouse, Wright; Hancocks, Stockin, Swinbourne, Wilshaw, Mullen

**West Bromwich Albion:** Heath; Rickaby, Millard; Dudley, Kennedy, Barlow; Griffin, Nicholls, Allen, Ryan, Lee

# CHARLTON ATHLETIC v. WOLVES

**Football League Division One at The Valley**

**Date:** Saturday 21 November 1953          **Attendance:** 43,807

---

High-flying Charlton were considered likely to throw a spanner in Wolves' works, but not this day. Wolves, back to full strength and encouraged by their victory over West Brom, started brightly, their power-play opening up the Addicks' defence on a number of occasions. However, it was Charlton that had the better of the opening exchanges, creating a number of good chances.

Fortunately for the visitors, in the early portion of this game centre forward Eddie Firmani was having an off day. It wasn't until the 24th minute, when Cyril Hammond lost his footing before he could clear the ball, that Wolves got the breakthrough they sought. Peter Broadbent was on hand to capitalise and open the scoring for Wanderers with a fine goal, crashing an unstoppable shot past Sam Bartram in the Addicks' goal.

Early in the second half, Johnny Hancocks' right-wing run picked up speed as he cut inside to score a marvellous goal with a tremendous cross-shot from an extremely tight angle; a typical Hancocks thunderbolt and a definite show-stealer. Roy Swinbourne threatened to grab another for Wolves when former England goalkeeper Sam Bartram made a mess of a clearance. The Charlton goalie advanced far beyond his 18-yard line and ended up pushing the ball straight to the Wolves centre forward. Fortunately for the home side, Derek Ufton was alert to the situation and prevented what looked like a certain goal.

Bill Shorthouse and Billy Wright were keeping Eddie Firmani and his fellow forwards very quiet, leading Wolves' defence in a calm and assured performance. Slater too had a great game, and with Bert Williams' positive handling Wolves looked very good indeed. The forwards were creative and dangerous, with Hancocks allowed a free role that saw him wandering all over the field, from where his shoot-on-sight policy produced some exciting moments. Centre forward Roy Swinbourne's excellent play certainly deserved at least one goal. However, it was his strike partner Dennis Wilshaw who got closest when his fierce shot scraped the top of the Charlton crossbar. Broadbent's all-action display almost wrested the star-turn tag from Hancocks, but not quite.

With this hard-fought win, Wolves extended their unbeaten run to 16 matches, still within a point of League leaders West Brom and 4 points ahead of third-placed Huddersfield.

There was no change at the top of the table following Albion's 6-1 thrashing of Cardiff City at The Hawthorns. Ronnie Allen banged in four goals, twice as many as Johnny Nicholls.

The local newspapers broke the story that Aston Villa had made a bid to sign Bill Baxter and Les Smith. The fans hoped that Smith would stay, despite, like Baxter, being restricted to the occasional outing because of injury or international call up.

A catastrophe of enormous proportions hit English football when the 1952 Olympic Champions Hungary humbled Billy Wright's England 6-3 at Wembley on the afternoon of Wednesday 25

---

**Charlton Athletic 0**

**Wolves 2**

*Broadbent (24)*

*Hancocks (54)*

# CHARLTON ATHLETIC v. WOLVES

Action from Charlton v. Wolves at The Valley. Bert Williams punches the ball from Eddie Firmani of Charlton.

November 1953. Nandor Hidegkuti scored a hat-trick, Ferenc Puskas got two and Josef Bozsik grabbed the other. England's scorers were Jackie Sewell, Stan Mortenson and Alf Ramsey with a penalty.

England: Merrick; Ramsey, Eckersley; Wright (Capt.), Johnston, Dickinson; Matthews, Taylor (E), Mortenson, Sewell, Robb.

Hungary: Grosics; Buzansky, Lantos; Bozsik, Lorant, Zakarias; Budai, Kocsis, Hidegkuti, Puskas, Czibor.

Reputedly, following this England humiliation, one so-called football 'expert' was so shaken that he called Stan Cullis to ask what changes he intended to make to Wolves' training sessions. 'None,' Stan emphatically replied. Cullis considered his methods to be equal to those anywhere in the world. In December 1954 he would be proved right, when seven of the Hungarian eleven that walloped England played for the Honved team who were beaten 3-2 by Wolves under the famous Molineux floodlights.

Obviously, the England team needed to include a greater number of Wolves players, specifically: Williams, Slater, Hancocks, Broadbent, Swinbourne, Wilshaw and Mullen.

On 23 May 1954, six months after the Wembley debacle, England made seven changes to the team to face Hungary in Budapest, Billy Wright again captaining the side. This time they lost 7-1, England's solitary goal being scored by Ivor Broadis. Like I said, they really should have drafted in a few more Wolves players.

England: Merrick; Staniforth, Byrne; Wright (Capt.), Owen, Dickinson; Harris (P), Sewell, Jezzard, Broadis, Finney.

Three days after the humiliating Wembley defeat, Billy Wright had to get back to the League programme.

On 26 November wing half Bill Baxter was transferred to Aston Villa, and hopefully got his wish for more first-team football.

---

**Charlton Athletic:** Bartram; Lock, Ellis; Fenton, Ufton, Hammond; Hurst, O'Linn, Firmani, Evans, Kiernan

**Wolves:** Williams; Short, Pritchard; W.J. Slater, Shorthouse, Wright; Hancocks, Broadbent, Swinbourne, Wilshaw, Mullen

# WOLVES V. SHEFFIELD WEDNESDAY

**Football League Division One at Molineux**

**Date:** Saturday 28 November 1953          **Attendance:** 35,154

Now it was the turn of Sheffield's other club to be on the end of a Wolves walloping as Wanderers preserved their 100% home record, but not before the visitors, prompted by inside left Jackie Sewell, who had scored one of England's goals against the Hungarians, had shocked the home side into action by taking an early lead. The game was only 6 minutes old when Dennis Woodhead rounded off a good Wednesday move with a smartly taken goal. Sewell threw over a long cross-field ball to Wednesday's left-winger, who cut inside Short to beat Williams with an excellently placed shot. That was the last thing the Owls should have done. Wolves now turned up the power with Johnny Hancocks playing quite magnificently.

On 12 minutes, following good work by Broadbent and Wilshaw, the little winger smashed a seemingly unstoppable shot at the Wednesday goal, which keeper Bryan Ryalls managed to keep out, but couldn't hold. When the ball tumbled out of his hands, there was Dennis Wilshaw, first to the ball to prod it home.

Bert Williams was equal to anything the Owls could throw his way, pulling off a couple of excellent saves to help Wolves maintain their dominance. The score surprisingly stayed at 1-1 until the 40th minute, when Hancocks scored a peach of a penalty to open up a little daylight between the two teams.

The second half saw Wolves extend their lead with two fine goals from Roy Swinbourne. His first came 4 minutes after the restart, Hancocks whipping in a lovely cross that Big Roy met perfectly. Then it was pretty much all over. Wednesday tried hard to avoid a thrashing, and they did well to contain Wolves' snarling forwards until 10 minutes from time, when Hancocks ran onto a sweet pass to blast the ball at the Sheffield goal. Ryalls again got his hands in the way to save, but unfortunately for him, up popped Swinbourne to crown a fine performance with his second goal of the afternoon.

The whole team were playing quite brilliantly, creating chance after chance, the defence giving a flawlessly fabulous performance, particularly in the second half. Hancocks set up two more opportunities for Wilshaw, who on another day would have tucked at least one of them away. Then it was Broadbent's turn to miss a sitter, and in the dying minutes Ryalls dived to save Mullen's effort from point-blank range. At times, one might have been excused for running out of suitable superlatives to describe Wolves' inventive play. There hadn't been as much trademark wing-to-wing passing after the break, but what was on show was wonderful to watch. Above all, it was Hancocks that epitomised all that is good in football. His tireless runs caused havoc in the visitor's defence throughout the 90 minutes; prompting this great victory. Wolves' fans were jubilant.

---

**Wolves 4**
*Wilshaw (12)*
*Hancocks (penalty) (40)*
*Swinbourne 2 (49 and 80)*

**Sheffield Wednesday 1**
*Woodhead (6)*

# WOLVES v. SHEFFIELD WEDNESDAY

Wolves skipper Billy Wright in action for England

At their Molineux fortress Wolves had now won 14 consecutive games, and were unbeaten in 17. Unfortunately for Wanderers, Albion had emerged from their encounter with Manchester City at Maine Road with a hard-won 3-2 victory to stay top by 1 point, courtesy of goals from Lee, Allen and Nicholls.

**Wolves:** Williams; Short, Pritchard; W.J. Slater, Shorthouse, Wright; Hancocks, Broadbent, Swinbourne, Wilshaw, Mullen

**Sheffield Wednesday:** Ryalls; Conwell, Curtis; Gannon, O'Donnell, Davies; Finney, Quixall, Jordon, Sewell, Woodhead

# TOTTENHAM HOTSPUR *v.* WOLVES

**Football League Division One at White Hart Lane**

**Date:** Saturday 5 December 1953          **Attendance:** 48,164

Wolves' recent record at White Hart Lane was nothing to inspire the fans' confidence that their magnificent run would continue, and when Spurs opened up the first half, the signs were ominous to say the least. Having said that, for the first 25 minutes of this game Wolves' defenders, despite being troubled by the slippery surface, were certainly grabbing the chance to show what they could do; they had to. However, in the 26th minute they were temporarily powerless to prevent inside right Les Bennett from opening the scoring for Tottenham with a close-range header. Fortunately they managed to hold out until the interval.

In the second half it was a different story, as Wolves turned on another power-play performance in England's capital city to make it three wins in three visits in the season thus far. First, it was reliable Dennis Wilshaw with a neat diving header from Hancocks' perfect cross for the equaliser in the 53rd minute. Less than a minute later, Peter Broadbent stunned the already fairly silent home crowd. Jimmy Mullen sent in a teasing cross which Wolves' number eight expertly flick-headed past Ted Ditchburn in the Tottenham goal. Wolves were fighting hard for every ball and winning most when their anticipated march to victory was put on hold.

Spurs' equaliser was the result of a glaring mistake made by the match officials when an offside Len Duquemin pulled the scores level. Wanderers' defence made the age-old mistake of not playing to the whistle. Every one of them stopped and turned in expectation to the referee, their appeals waved away with disdain.

With time running out, Johnny Hancocks, who had teased and tormented the Spurs back line all game, produced a moment of outstanding football – as deft a piece of ball artistry as one is ever likely to see. The little number seven managed to reach a ball on the Spurs byline that was otherwise going nowhere but out and dragged it inside onto his left foot to sidestep Alf Ramsey and the onrushing Withers before finishing with great aplomb from the most acute angle imaginable. This was one of those all-in-one movements, incredible skill preceding one of Johnny's trademark crashing shots, this time with his left foot. The ball rocketed past Ted Ditchburn, who probably thought he had it covered, passing through the tightest of gaps between the post and the big Spurs 'keeper's body. With less than 10 minutes to go, this proved to be the goal that fired Wolves to the top of the table for the first time that season, following Portsmouth's 3-2 victory at The Hawthorns.

This was a game in which Wolves seemed to introduce a more deliberate offside element to their game. One would hope that if they were to persist with this tactic that they would practise it in training more often than they appeared to have done prior to this match. Apart from the Hancocks masterclass, Wright and Slater were once again outstanding, and with Broadbent demonstrating his

| Tottenham Hotspur 2 | Wolves 3 |
|---|---|
| *Bennett (26)* | *Wilshaw (53)* |
| *Duquemin (56)* | *Broadbent (54)* |
| | *Hancocks (80)* |

61

# TOTTENHAM HOTSPUR v. WOLVES

*Above left:* Wolves' goalkeeper Bert Williams covers his post and the ball goes over the bar during Wolves' game with Spurs at White Hart Lane.

*Above right:* Wolves' goalkeeper Bert Williams dives as once again the ball goes over the bar during Wolves' game with Spurs at White Hart Lane.

pedigree, especially his slinky body-swerve where he seemed to glide past defenders, all the omens looked good for Wolves. Incidentally, the Spurs team included a couple of players later to become even more famous: Alf Ramsey as England's 1966 World Cup-winning manager, and Bill Nicholson as manager of Spurs' 1961 Double-winning team.

Goals from Allen and Nicholls couldn't prevent Albion's faltering performance against Portsmouth, where they went down 3-2. This meant that Wolves went top of the League by 1 point. Eighteen games unbeaten! It was halfway through the season and Wolves' proud record read:

|        | PLD | W  | D | L | F  | A  | PTS |
|--------|-----|----|---|---|----|----|-----|
| Wolves | 21  | 14 | 5 | 2 | 54 | 29 | 33  |
| **Albion** | **21** | **15** | **2** | **4** | **58** | **28** | **32** |

Now Wolves had the benefit of a three-matches-at-home run to look forward to. First up, Burnley.

---

**Tottenham Hotspur:** Ditchburn; Ramsey, Withers; Nicholson, Clarke, Burgers; Walters, Bennett, Duquemin, Baily, MacClellan

**Wolves:** Williams; Short, Pritchard; W.J. Slater, Shorthouse, Wright; Hancocks, Broadbent, Swinbourne, Wilshaw, Mullen

# Wolves v. Burnley

Football League Division One at Molineux

**Date:** Saturday 12 December 1953         **Attendance:** 35,043

---

Well I guess like all good things, it had to end one day. Two brilliantly taken goals by Jim Holden coupled with the Burnley defence's never-say-die attitude robbed Wolves of the chance to extend their 100% home record. Its funny that Burnley were the team to halt Wanderers' 18-game unbeaten run, including 14 successive victories at Molineux, 5 last season and 9 this. Also funny was that Wolves' run was ended by the team that held the record for the longest unbeaten run in the First Division. In season 1920/21 they were unbeaten in 30 League games, although they did lose one along the way in the FA Cup.

Burnley played a nice thoughtful brand of football and thoroughly deserved their victory over Wolves on this grey Molineux day; they were one of the best outfits to visit Molineux for a long time. This shouldn't have been a surprise to Wolves, following the 4-1 defeat at the hands of the Clarets on the opening day of the season. The same forward line that scored those 4 goals once again had the home side's defence all over the shop.

The game kicked off at 2.15 p.m., promising to be a lively affair with Wanderers setting off like an express train. Wolves wanted revenge as well as wanting to remain leaders of the top division. At the forefront of a vicious onslaught on the Clarets' goal was Jimmy Mullen, who sent over a seemingly never-ending stream of dangerous crosses, mostly prompted by accurate down-wing passes from Billy Wright. Unfortunately, the Burnley defenders and centre half Cummings in particular gobbled each of them up before any Wolves' forward could reach them. Cummings' hold on Swinbourne was proving to be pretty watertight; however, Big Roy eventually managed to break free to send a marvellous snap-shot goalwards, only to see Thompson acrobatically tip the ball over the crossbar.

Burnley escaped rather luckily when Johnny Hancocks thumped a rare header against a post. After this the game quietened down for a spell with not much to report until just after the half-hour, when Cummings' long clearance upfield found centre forward Jim Holden. He cleverly controlled the ball and easily took it past Short before running on to fire Burnley in front. Wolves didn't take this affront lying down, and stormed back at the visitors without any success. The 1-0 scoreline at half-time was definitely not a true reflection of the pattern of the game. Everyone inside Molineux welcomed this 10-minute breather, such had been the cracking pace of the first 45 minutes.

The second period began as the first had ended with Wolves pounding away, only to be met with a stubborn and resolute defence. Then, 9 minutes after the restart another long-punted clearance, this time from Jimmy Adamson, found Holden in acres of space. In an almost carbon copy of his first goal, he flicked the ball past Bert Williams, who had raced out of his goal, to put his side two up. I don't think any one of the 35,000 crowd could quite believe it.

---

**Wolves 1**

*Hancocks (84)*

**Burnley 2**

*Holden 2 (31 and 54)*

# WOLVES v. BURNLEY

Peter Broadbent, Wolves.

Back onto the attack came Wolves, but try as they might they couldn't find the breakthrough their play so richly deserved. They seemed destined not to score. With only 6 minutes remaining, Wolves finally got one back through Johnny Hancocks, prompting an even more vicious bombardment on the Burnley goal. In the dying minutes, Swinbourne had a great chance to level the scores, but his shot skimmed the wrong side of a post to the great relief of the visitors.

Despite Wanderers' storming finish, it was not to be. The Clarets had once again kicked the wheels off Wolves' cart, upsetting the apples and breaking Wanderers' fans' hearts in the process. The Burnley players were generously applauded from the pitch by the home fans. Undoubtedly, they were one of the best outfits seen at Molineux that season, their close-marking, quick-tackling style mirrored that of Wolves, the only difference on the day being that they did everything just that bit better, and Wolves didn't have a Holden. Johnny Hancocks' goal put him level with Roy Swinbourne on 14 for the season to date, 1 less than Dennis Wilshaw.

Burnley's victory meant that Albion leapfrogged Wolves back to the top of the table on goal average following their 2-2 draw at Highbury. Both teams were now sitting on 33 points. Johnny Nicholls got both goals for Albion.

The draw for the third round of the FA Cup paired Wolves with Second Division Birmingham City at Molineux. The teams had never met in the Cup, although on 1 February 1890, Wolves had beaten their forebears, Small Heath, 2-1. Albion had drawn Chelsea at home, Villa would have to visit Arsenal, and Walsall had to travel to Lincoln.

---

**Wolves:** Williams; Short, Pritchard; W.J. Slater, Shorthouse, Wright; Hancocks, Stockin, Swinbourne, Wilshaw, Mullen

**Burnley:** Thompson; Aird, Mather; Adamson, Cummings, Attwell; Gray, McIlroy, Holden, Shannon, Pilkington

# WOLVES V. MANCHESTER CITY

**Football League Division One at Molineux**

**Date:** Saturday 19 December 1953          **Attendance:** 27,606

Another 2.15 p.m. kick-off, and a disappointingly low gate – the smallest to date – was blamed on two factors; one, obviously the Burnley defeat, and the other, the fact that Christmas was fast approaching and this was the last shopping Saturday before the holiday period. The concept of 24/7 shopping was unthought of in those days.

Manchester City were hoping for a better result than the corresponding game of the previous season, which they had lost by a staggering 7-3 margin. An unchanged Wolves side showed the sort of determination the fans were looking for.

Wanderers opened up with a series of attacks that resulted in good efforts by Hancocks and Swinbourne, both bringing impressive saves from Bert Trautmann in City's goal. Then Hancocks cheekily tricked Dave Ewing, but screwed his shot wide of the post when he looked odds-on to score. Next, it was Wilshaw's turn to test the big blond goalkeeper, who once again showed his pedigree with a world-class save. All this was in a spell of 20 or so minutes of barnstorming non-stop attacking. However, as had been witnessed all too frequently in the past, the home team needed a kick up the backside to spur them into goalscoring action.

A few minutes before the half-hour, the already edgy Molineux crowd were silenced by City's inside left Gordon Davies, who took his chance well, scoring a clever goal. City's left half Roy Paul kept probing for an opening and eventually got a telling ball out to Clarke, whose accurate cross was taken in his stride by Davies, before firing in a low drive that went in off Williams' hands. Manchester's right-half-cum-deep-lying centre forward Don Revie, the future controversial Leeds United and England manager, and his fellow half-backs Paul and Ewing and the outstanding Trautmann were still managing to thwart most of Wolves' early attacks, mostly by subduing Broadbent and Wilshaw.

Thankfully, Lady Luck intervened in the 36th minute when Sheffield referee Mr Murdock awarded Wolves a most welcome penalty when Wilshaw was brought down in the area. Johnny Hancocks thundered the ball past a helpless Bert Trautmann to bring his total for the season to 15, the same number as Wilshaw. Wolves' number seven then embarked upon a one-man onslaught on the big German's goal. He smashed shot after shot at the visitors' goal, but somehow the often-lucky Trautmann managed to save all of them. Half-time came and went with the score remaining 1-1.

After the break, Wolves' forwards improved, attacking with a lot more purpose and urgency. Trautmann miraculously kept out a stunning effort from Mullen; surely Wolves must score soon? The answer was yes, but it took the home side over a quarter of an hour of the second half to finally grab the lead. Inevitably, it was Dennis Wilshaw who got it on 62 minutes, his 16th of the season.

---

**Wolves 3**

*Hancocks 2 (penalty 36 and 89)*
*Wilshaw (62)*

**Manchester City 1**

*Davies (26)*

65

# WOLVES v. MANCHESTER CITY

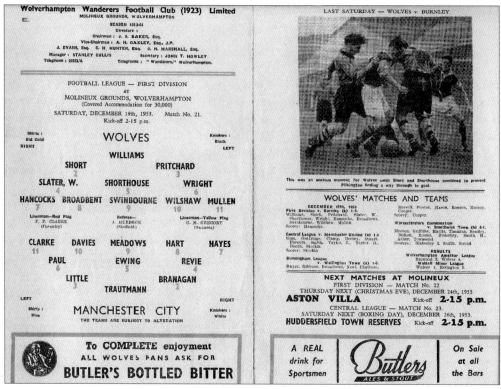

Team page – programme Wolves v. Manchester City.

Trautmann pushed out a lob from Broadbent to Wilshaw, who smacked the ball home with his left foot. Fittingly, it was Hancocks who wrapped it up for Wolves; the little winger scored with only a minute left on the clock, beating Trautmann to the ball before slamming it into City's net with his left peg. This was Wolves' first double of the season – and didn't they make hard work of it!

The race for the League title was beginning to hot up, and with it the excitement on both sides of the Black Country. Wolves and Albion supporters eagerly awaited each week's results to see if their team was the one sitting proudly at the top of England's Premier League.

The Baggies lost 2-1 to title contenders Bolton Wanderers, Paddy Ryan scoring their solitary goal, and so Wolves returned to the top spot with their win over Manchester City; this time they had a 2-point advantage.

The fans didn't have to wait long for the next match at Molineux, and this was another derby game, this time against Aston Villa.

---

**Wolves:** Williams; Short, Pritchard; W.J. Slater, Shorthouse, Wright; Hancocks, Broadbent, Swinbourne, Wilshaw, Mullen

**Manchester City:** Trautmann; Branagan, Little; Revie, Ewing, Paul; Hayes, Hart, Meadows, Davies, Clarke

# Wolves v. Aston Villa

**Football League Division One at Molineux**

**Date:** Thursday 24 December 1953          **Attendance:** 40,536

---

The result of this derby game was definitely not the best start to Wolves' Christmas and New Year programme. Wolves' fans packed into Molineux expecting their team to continue their winning ways at home, particularly after the agony of the disappointment against Burnley and the ecstasy of the win over Man City. Sadly, Bert Williams wouldn't make the line-up after being injured in that game, Nigel Sims deputising. Villa named ex-Wolf Bill Baxter captain for the day against his former club, and boy did he set out to show Wolves what they had lost. Cheered onto the pitch, he won the toss and then gave a tireless and exemplary display of dynamic wing half play that helped Villa pull off a surprise victory over the new League leaders. Prompted by Baxter, Villa started the game with a real fire in their bellies that had Wolves on the rack for long periods of a game that had plenty of excitement, without an abundance of outstanding football. Although, in truth, despite a lot of huffing and puffing, Villa never managed to trouble Sims in Wolves' goal.

Naturally, it was Hancocks that thumped in Wolves' first shot of the game, which unfortunately was blocked. Then Slater burst through a couple of Villa defenders to take Swinbourne's pass, his delicate lob surprising Keith Jones, who had come too far off his line. Luckily for him the ball landed just behind the bar. Mullen sent Hancocks clear resulting in another thunderbolt, which smacked Vinall full in the face. The Villa full-back needed a lot of wet-sponge attention before he could continue. Villa pressed home a number of attacks that brought them nothing apart from a scramble in Wanderers' goalmouth. This was after Hancocks had somehow allowed Swinbourne's pass to bounce off his foot. As if this wasn't bad enough, then the winger blasted a Wilshaw pass a foot wide of the near post.

After much toing and froing, it was the home side that took the lead, and much against the early run of play it was. Before this, Wolves had almost scored when Slater slid a nice ball out to Hancocks, who swapped a couple of passes with Broadbent before Wolves' number eight floated over a high cross that Swinbourne headed powerfully down, but the Villa goalkeeper saved well. A few minutes later, an almost identical move brought the goal Wolves' fans hoped for, this time it was Hancocks that centred for Dennis Wilshaw to direct an excellent header well wide of Jones to put Wolves one up.

Anticipation is a fickle bedfellow, as Wolves were about to demonstrate to their army of fans who now expected their team to get on top and pulverise the Villains from the second city. Apart from a flurry of quick-fire football from Wolves following the goal, which included Hancocks nodding a yard wide from Mullen's cross, it was the Villa players that rolled their sleeves up and got stuck in, renewing the ferocity of their attacks, as if to prove that Wolves' goal had merely flattered to

---

**Wolves 1**

*Wilshaw (22)*

**Aston Villa 2**

*Dixon (55)*

*McParland (80)*

67

deceive. Then, following some clever footwork from Dixon, the excellent Parkes collided badly with Shorthouse and needed treatment. He spent the rest of the half, all but the final 2 minutes, hobbling on the right-wing, Gibson having slotted into his right-back berth. That's when he had to be carried from the field by the Villa trainer and Dick Dorset, but not before he had limped in to send a stinging low-drive that Sims did well to keep out.

Baxter was proving to be the main destroyer of Wolves' creativity, putting in great tackles on Broadbent and Mullen that the crowd applauded loudly. He then whipped in a smart free-kick that had Sims stretching to tip the ball over. Wolves responded with their best attack of the game. Some accurate play saw the ball reach Hancocks, who smashed a left-footer just over the bar.

On 40 minutes Wolves won a free-kick. Hancocks took aim and sent in a swerving thunderbolt that took Jones by surprise but, somehow, the Villa 'keeper managed to recover to punch the ball over. With a little more luck, Hancocks could have scored five or six by now.

Villa stormed back at Wolves, and debutant Peter McParland broke clean away. Out rushed Sims to beat out the young Irishman's shot from 8 yards for a corner. 1-0 to Wolves at half-time, and there was hardly time to draw breath before the two combatants renewed the fight. Once again Villa forced Wanderers onto the back foot, McParland and Dixon looking dangerous, with brave Parkes adding to the pressure with some determined work. Villa were really up for this game and went close with a number of good efforts. Having said this, it still took the visitors a long time to get the goal that their excellent play deserved.

Since the restart, they had continued to press Wolves' defence, and in the 55th minute grabbed the equaliser through Johnny Dixon; it was no more than they deserved. From a corner, the ball fizzed about a bit before reaching Dixon and, although he hesitated, he still managed to sweep the ball wide of Sims' outstretched arm through a crowd of players. During this prolonged spell of Villa pressure, Wolves' forwards were being effectively subdued by the Villa defenders, with Hancocks and Mullen rarely being allowed to show what they could do. Swinbourne too was held in check by Moss, and even when opportunities were presented to the lads in gold, all contrived to miss the target.

Eventually, a glimmer of hope came from a wonderful sweeping eight-man move that ended disappointingly with Wilshaw heading tamely into Jones' arms. Then prompted by Wright, it was Wolves again on top: Wilshaw to Mullen, then a quick cross from which Hancocks flashed a header just over. Seconds later, Slater powerfully headed the ball from a corner into Jones' arms. Straight after this, Mullen whipped over a centre that Hancocks volleyed narrowly wide, and following this Jones was lucky to stop a Hancocks shot with his left foot. Great chances, but Wolves couldn't stick any of them away. Mind you, it could still have gone either way.

In the 78th minute Dixon sent Thompson clear, but Sims was equal to the task, stopping his shot with some panache. In the end, it was Villa's name that came out of the hat. Harry Parkes was still limping along the right-wing, and in the 80th minute conned a throw-in out of the referee near Wolves' corner post. Thompson squared the ball, and in the ensuing mêlée, Villa's left-winger Peter McParland lashed it into Wolves' net.

The home side woke up and threw everything at the Villa goal, but it was once again a case of too little, too late, and Wolves had lost again at Molineux, their second defeat in three games. This was certainly a result to forget as quickly as possible; Wolves had to play Villa again in two days' time. Finishing-wise, Wolves almost couldn't do anything right, squandering chance after chance.

# Wolves v. Aston Villa

Where was the power-play? Where was the fighting spirit the fans demanded from their team? Perhaps the players had eaten their Christmas dinner a day early, who knows?

Fortunately, Wolves were still top of the League because Albion hadn't yet played their first Christmas game.

The top five looked like this:
    First: Wolves 35 points from 24 games
    Second: Albion 33 points from 23 games
    Third: Huddersfield 30 points from 23 games
    Fourth: Burnley 30 points from 23 games
    Fifth: Bolton 26 points from 22 games

The euphoria of the faithful, if that's what you could call it, was unhappily only temporary. It quickly evaporated as, on Christmas Day morning, the Baggies walloped Liverpool 5-2 at The Hawthorns to go top on goal average and give themselves a nice Christmas present. Nicholls, Griffin (2), Barlow and Allen got the goals. Both Black Country teams would be away on Boxing Day, Albion at Liverpool and Wolves at the Villa, so it was a case of who would be least affected by Christmas cheer. At least Wolves had an extra day to recover.

**Wolves:** Sims; Short, Pritchard; W.J. Slater, Shorthouse, Wright; Hancocks, Broadbent, Swinbourne, Wilshaw, Mullen
**Aston Villa:** Jones; Parkes, Vinall; Baxter, Moss (F), Moss (A); Gibson, Blanchflower, Dixon, Thompson, McParland

# ASTON VILLA *v.* WOLVES

**Football League Division One at Villa Park**

**Date:** Saturday 26 December 1953          **Attendance:** 48,560

---

What a difference a day, or two, makes. After almost ruining most Wolves' fans' Christmas dinner, Wanderers returned to winning ways with an all-out display of power-packed attacking play. Hancocks and Mullen were back to their best, terrorising Villa's full-backs Stan Lynn and Vinall and, along with Swinbourne, Wilshaw and Broadbent, giving the Villa defence a real pounding. They really should have scored two or three in the first 20 minutes, but they didn't. Instead, as is so often the case, it was the team under the cosh that got the first breakthrough.

Almost on the half-hour, and completely against the play, in one of the home side's rare forays upfield, Villa grabbed the first goal of the game. The move was started by Moss with a long pass to inside left Tommy Thompson, who set off on a 40-yard run jinking past two Wolves defenders, who both expected him to square the ball to Johnny Dixon, before calmly slotting the ball past Sims.

This was a completely different match to the Christmas Eve encounter. This time Villa were facing a much more determined Wolves' team than at Molineux. Despite putting up an initial resolute barrier, Villa's defence eventually broke, and 3 minutes later Johnny Hancocks crashed in one of his characteristic shots that deflected past the stranded Villa goalkeeper Keith Jones off Bill Baxter's boot as he vainly tried to kick the ball away.

In between Wolves' incessant attacks, Villa put up a brave fight and might have surprised the visitors. Dixon almost managed to divert the ball past Sims, who also saved a good effort from Moss with his foot. Soon after the restart, Dennis Wilshaw scored what looked to be a fine goal that was ruled out by a myopically challenged linesman who believed that Peter Broadbent was in an offside position and interfering with play. Then Broadbent shot just over, following a move that was almost a carbon copy of Wilshaw's earlier effort.

Wolves were now completely on top. Vinall kicked a Broadbent header off the line just before Roy Swinbourne rattled the Villa crossbar with an excellent effort, and Hancocks fired in several cannonball shots that either narrowly missed or were dealt with by Jones. Despite this onslaught, it took Wolves until the 88th minute to get the winner. Hancocks' centre flew over everyone's head and, after a mad scramble in the Villa goalmouth, the ball came out to Jimmy Mullen, who centred. Then, once again, there was Dennis Wilshaw, leaping high above the defenders to head the ball home into the top corner, giving Jones no chance. There was no time for Villa to recover from the pounding they had taken, allowing Wolves to ease away the memory of the Christmas Eve defeat from the minds of their fans with a thoroughly deserved victory.

The news that Albion had only managed a 0-0 draw at Anfield heartened Wolves' supporters, whose team were now entering the New Year on top of the League by a single point. Those New

---

**Aston Villa 1**

*Thompson (28)*

**Wolves 2**

*Hancocks (31)*

*Wilshaw (88)*

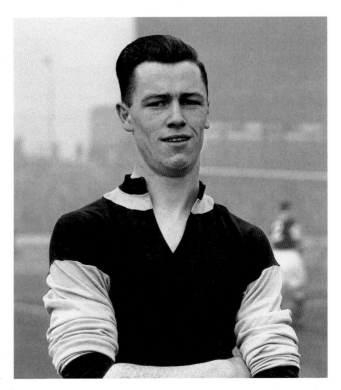

Peter McParland, Aston Villa.

Year celebrations tasted very sweet indeed.

|              | PLD | W  | D  | L | F  | A  | PTS |
|--------------|-----|----|----|---|----|----|-----|
| **Wolves**   | 25  | 16 | 5  | 4 | 61 | 35 | 37  |
| Albion       | 25  | 16 | 4  | 5 | 66 | 34 | 36  |
| Huddersfield | 25  | 13 | 7  | 5 | 45 | 27 | 33  |
| Burnley      | 25  | 16 | 0  | 9 | 55 | 42 | 32  |
| Man Utd      | 25  | 9  | 10 | 6 | 46 | 35 | 28  |

Note the number of goals scored by Wolves and Albion compared to the other three teams; a tribute to the brand of attacking football being played by the two Black Country rivals.

Now it was off to South Wales to face the scourge of goalkeepers everywhere, big Trevor Ford, who had transferred to Cardiff City from Sunderland earlier in the season.

---

**Aston Villa:** Jones; Lynn, Vinall; Baxter, Martin, Moss (A); Gibson, Blanchflower, Dixon, Thompson, McParland
**Wolves:** Sims; Short, Pritchard; W.J. Slater, Shorthouse, Wright; Hancocks, Broadbent, Swinbourne, Wilshaw, Mullen

# CARDIFF CITY V. WOLVES

Football League Division One at Ninian Park

**Date:** Saturday 2 January 1954          **Attendance:** 47,113

Nigel Sims retained his place in Wolves' goal, as Bert Williams hadn't recovered from injury in time to face his old sparring partner, Welsh international centre forward Trevor Ford. These two had had some real ding-dong battles in the past. In the absence of the injured Short, Billy Wright was once again asked to switch to right-back where he had done so well at Liverpool in September, Ron Flowers coming in at left half.

The game kicked-off at 2.30 p.m. on what turned out to be a nice day in more ways than one. Wolves turned in a first-class performance which thoroughly deserved the points, as well as bringing them their second double of the season. Cardiff's burly centre forward began in typical fiery fashion, bustling his way through the visitors' defence to fire in a couple of useful early shots. The first Nigel Sims turned brilliantly over the bar and the second flew a foot over before Bill Shorthouse managed to get the upper hand over the big number nine in their bruising duel. Shorthouse was commanding, particularly in the air.

The real fireworks were at the other end of the pitch, where Wolves were launching a series of dangerous attacks against a team far too reliant on the offside trap. One of these attacks resulted in Roy Swinbourne getting his first goal since his brace against Sheffield Wednesday on 28 November; amazingly, Roy had gone five games without scoring. The goal spurred Wolves to double their efforts and, 17 minutes later, a well-deserved second goal came. This time it was the trusty boot of Dennis Wilshaw that did the damage. He cleverly sprung the home side's poor offside trap before racing through to score.

Wolves' wingers Mullen and Hancocks were using their trademark crossfield balls to great effect, opening up the Cardiff defence on several occasions, and of course, Hancocks fired in a series of cannonball shots that unfortunately either bounced off defenders or missed the goal. Surprisingly, the score stayed at 2-0 to Wolves at the break, Wolves' only problem being the fact that Bill Slater had picked up a very painful knock.

After the interval, Wolves seemed to ease off the gas a bit and on the hour were caught napping when Cliff Nugent darted in to give the Welshmen a glimmer of hope with a fine goal. Now was the time for Wolves' defence to put on a show of dogged determination, and they did just that. Faced with some excellent defending, in which Wright and Shorthouse were outstanding, the home side's attack sputtered and eventually fizzled out, Wright completely shutting out Edwards.

In Wolves' goal, Nigel Sims put in as cool a performance as is ever likely to be seen, cutting out crosses and cleanly taking every ball that had the temerity to stray into his area with commensurate ease. Meek surrender followed. Johnny Hancocks' brilliant 81st-minute goal put the seal on a great

| Cardiff City 1 | Wolves 3 |
|---|---|
| *Nugent (60)* | *Swinbourne (20)* |
| | \ *Wilshaw (37)* |
| | *Hancocks (81)* |

72

Les Smith.

victory. In truth Wolves' capricious forwards allowed themselves to stray too often into offside positions, particularly Roy Swinbourne, and this was most evident in the second half. Young Ron Flowers did okay, but on another day his sometimes hesitant approach might have been punished. Fortunately, Roy Pritchard was there to back him up with a sterling display.

Wolves were still top despite Albion's 3-2 hard-fought win over Preston at The Hawthorns, Allen (2) and Nicholls again the scorers. It was a close call that saw the Baggies have to struggle to get both points. Nicholls had now scored 24 goals since the start of the season, and Ronnie Allen had notched 22.

The rumour on the streets was that Wolves' utility winger Les Smith was a target for Burnley as well as Aston Villa, and that the £15,000 transfer fee would make him a Burnley player within the next few days. The fans would be sorry to see Les go. Anyway, it was now time for a break from the League programme as the third round of the FA Cup loomed large. Sixty-four hopeful teams would contest the round that many believe to be one of the greatest days in the English football calendar.

For this match Wolves unpopularly decided to put up the price of entry. Waterloo Road centre seats would cost 8s 6d, 7s for the wings and the Molineux Street Stand, enclosures 3s 6d (boys 1s 9d), North Bank 2s (boys 1s), and South Bank 1s 9d (boys 9d). Girls didn't even get a mention!

---

**Cardiff City:** Howells; Rutter, Stitfall; Baker, Montgomery, Sullivan; Thomas, Nugent, Ford, Northcote, Edwards

**Wolves:** Sims; Wright, Pritchard; W.J. Slater, Shorthouse, Flowers; Hancocks, Broadbent, Swinbourne, Wilshaw, Mullen

# WOLVES V. BIRMINGHAM CITY

**FA Cup Third Round Tie at Molineux**

**Date:** Saturday 9 January 1954          **Attendance:** 36,784

---

On their day, Wolves could beat any League team in the country, but this was different, it was FA Cup third round day, when so often in the past many big scalps had been taken by so-called football minnows. Would Wolves be confident? Could the Brummies raise their game like they had in the previous year's competition when they had bravely reached the sixth round? They were obviously Cup fighters. All was to be revealed shortly. When the names came out of the hat, manager Bob Brocklebank and his Second Division Birmingham City players must have felt themselves unlucky to be drawn away to the League leaders. Mind you, they certainly didn't play as if they were overawed. Ably led by Peter Murphy, they out-thought and outplayed a very below-par Wolves team that lacked the necessary fight.

The pitch had been covered with frost overnight and was still bone-hard despite a bout of early-morning rain. Both goalmouths had been protected overnight with covers, as was the custom at Molineux, and so weren't too bad. Considering this was a Cup game between two fairly local teams, the attendance was disappointingly below 40,000. Short returned at right-back for Wolves, enabling Billy Wright to return to left half and so, apart from Nigel Sims making his FA Cup debut in goal, Wanderers were able to field their strongest side. Birmingham were not as fortunate; dynamic centre forward Ted Purdon had been transferred to Sunderland on the Thursday before the game.

Taking his place for his first game of the season would be a young twenty-year-old ex-Army Heavyweight Boxing Champion, Jackie Lane. Lane, who incidentally wore contact lenses, had only played 5 games during the previous season, partly because he was serving in the Royal Artillery, and because of Purdon's excellent form. Murphy had missed a few games with a nasty toe injury, but was determined to play in this game. Likewise, Green and Smith had been suffering from colds all week and were doubtful until the morning of the game.

The weather may have been lousy, but actually, Wolves didn't start too badly. They pushed the visitors back with a couple of incisive moves that brought the best out of England's current number one goalkeeper Gil Merrick, before taking the lead in the 10th minute with a super goal from Dennis Wilshaw. Following a nice move, Wilshaw drew Merrick from his goal and ended with a superbly struck rising-drive that caressed the underside of the bar on its way into the net.

Thoughts of 'this was going to be easy' must have crept into the minds of Wolves' players and fans alike, but they should have remembered, this was the Cup. Birmingham stormed back, snarling, teeth bared in the way that a wild animal would turn to attack if provoked. A ferocious bombardment that saw Astall and Lane go close with long-range efforts brought the equaliser after only 2 minutes' more play. The Blues' goal was scored with some panache by ex-Wolf Ken Rowley,

---

**Wolves 1**

*Wilshaw (10)*

**Birmingham City 2**

*Rowley (12)*

*Murphy (76)*

who had been transferred to the Blues in 1950 after playing just 3 games for Wolves' first team between 28 January and 4 February 1950, two of these in the FA Cup. He raced through a gap in Wolves' defence to beat Sims with a fine shot. The City fans thought their team unlucky to go in level at half-time. Wolves' fans thought the opposite, especially as a great attempt by Swinbourne had hit the Brummies' post.

Blues began the second half where they had left off, attacking a team that bore no resemblance whatsoever to a team that was leading the League. Few players seemed up for this game, and despite having a good share of the ball in the second 45 minutes, failed to fashion much in the way of clear-cut chances. All too often, Wanderers' so-slow players were caught in possession and too easily robbed by the City lads; they lacked fight. Naturally, the result of this half-hearted approach was to put the home defence under intense pressure.

Again, it was Astall and Lane that looked most likely to score, ably backed up by some excellent play from wing halves Boyd and Warhurst. Eventually Birmingham got their just rewards. It came from a sudden breakaway, when the ever-classy Peter Murphy slotted home what proved to be the winner.

A late injury to Bill Shorthouse forced Wolves to reshuffle their back line, with big Bill having to see out the game on the right wing. From a rare Wolves corner, Dennis Wilshaw tried to salvage a little pride for the home team with a late effort that had Merrick scrambling to make a save, but it was not to be, Wolves just couldn't find the spark that would ignite their game. Wanderers didn't show any measure of superiority, or was it that Birmingham showed no inferiority? Well, at least now Wolves could concentrate on the League. As it turned out, this game was to be the start of a near-disastrous run of defeats for Wolves.

The Baggies were a little fortunate to beat Chelsea 1-0 at home, courtesy of an own goal, to progress to the next round, when Stan Rickaby's thunderous shot was deflected passed his own 'keeper by none other than Ron Greenwood, the future England manager.

Back to the League the following Saturday: Wolves would entertain the Gunners at Molineux and Albion were scheduled to face Spurs at White Hart Lane; Black Country versus North London.

---

**Wolves:** Sims; Short, Pritchard; W.J. Slater, Shorthouse, Wright; Hancocks, Broadbent, Swinbourne, Wilshaw, Mullen

**Birmingham City:** Merrick; Hall, Green; Boyd, Smith, Warhurst; Astall, Rowley, Lane, Murphy, Govan

# Wolves v. Arsenal

Football League Division One at Molineux

Date: Saturday 16 January 1954       Attendance: 45,974

---

Bert Williams was back in League action. However, Bill Shorthouse would miss this one, so Billy Wright took over for his first game at centre half and captain, his left-half berth being filled by young Ron Flowers.

The game kicked off at 2.45 p.m. and it didn't take long before Dame Controversy paid a visit. With more than a little assistance from the match officials, Arsenal cheekily took the lead in the 9th minute. Milton found Holton down the middle with a neat pass and the big number nine, who, by the way, looked decidedly offside, then slipped a nice ball through for little Jimmy Logie to score with a close-range effort. This was after Wolves had opened up brightly.

Following the goal, Arsenal were forced into backs-to-the-wall defensive mode as Wolves released their own version of Armageddon, but somehow managed to rush their finishing when a little more steadiness might have brought the right result. Ron Flowers nearly grabbed an equaliser within minutes of the Gunners' goal, then Hancocks and Swinbourne both went close.

It's a wonder that the woodwork surrounding the visitors' goal didn't collapse, so frequently did ferocious shots cannon off it. Roy Swinbourne hit two shots that banged off the crossbar, sandwiched between two equally thunderous efforts by Flowers and Hancocks that achieved the same result. It was almost impossible to believe the charmed life that the Gunners' goal seemed to have, but it was true: they still led by the only goal of the first half. In the Arsenal goal, Jack Kelsey had produced a first-class display of agility, even if he rode his luck a few times; some of his stops were out of this world, particularly a couple of brilliant saves from Wilshaw and Hancocks.

The second half once again saw attack after attack from Wolves frustrated as the ball either struck the Arsenal woodwork or various parts of defenders' anatomies only to rebound each time to safety; talk about luck! Wolves were having none of it, whereas Arsenal were having loads of the stuff.

Johnny Hancocks took a nasty bang on the eyebrow, which caused him to have to leave the field for treatment; he returned with three stitches in the wound. Then disaster was confirmed 5 minutes before time when Arsenal broke away on the right through Don Roper, who had switched wings with Milton. His well-flighted centre was delicately flicked past Williams by the head of Doug Lishman. This was only Arsenal's second serious attack of a game in which, goals aside, Bert Williams wasn't troubled all afternoon. There's no justice.

Kelsey on the other hand was kept as busy as a bee by Wolves' mercurial forwards; he was quite literally magnificent. How could Wolves lose this one? They were better than the Gunners in every department, apart from in goal. This was Wanderers' fourth home defeat in five games, and the first

---

**Wolves 0**            **Arsenal 2**

*Logie (9)*

*Lishman (85)*

Arsenal 1952/53 League Champions.

time since December 1952 that they had failed to score in a match at Molineux. It was also only the second time they hadn't scored in a match that season; they and we deserved much better.

To top it all, Albion beat Tottenham 1-0 at White Hart Lane with a Ronnie Allen goal to regain the League's top spot by 1 point.

|  | PLD | W | D | L | F | A | PTS |
|---|---|---|---|---|---|---|---|
| Albion | 27 | 18 | 4 | 5 | 70 | 36 | 40 |
| **Wolves** | **27** | **17** | **5** | **5** | **64** | **38** | **39** |

**Wolves:** Williams; Short, Pritchard; W.J. Slater, Wright, Flowers; Hancocks, Broadbent, Swinbourne, Wilshaw, Mullen

**Arsenal:** Kelsey; Wills, Wade; Dickson, Dodgin, Forbes; Milton, Logie, Holton, Lishman, Roper

# Portsmouth v. Wolves

**Football League Division One at Fratton Park**

**Date:** Saturday 23 January 1954       **Attendance:** 35,321

---

Wolves were forced into a couple of team changes. Billy Wright moved to left-back in place of Roy Pritchard, who Cullis had decided to rest, Bill Shorthouse returning at centre half. Peter Broadbent moved to inside left in place of Dennis Wilshaw, who had been granted a leave of absence so that he could be with his critically ill father, and Norman Deeley took over at number eight. So it was with a bit of a strange line-up that Wolves took the field on the South Coast seeking to return to winning ways.

Lady Luck was still not smiling on Wolves, in a game that heaped more woe on their shoulders in the 8th minute of this match. The across-goal-area run of Reid and Shorthouse unsighted Bert Williams, resulting in the 'keeper being beaten by the high bounce of Jimmy Dickinson's hopeful lob, which had followed good work by the electrifying Harris on Pompey's right wing. It was a cruel blow for Wolves who, although not actually lacklustre, certainly hadn't the sparkle they had in abundance in the first half of the season. Apart from one wonderful lob from Johnny Hancocks which went inside the post and which Wolves felt had crossed the line for the equaliser by at least a foot, there wasn't much to report. Talk about frustration.

In the second half, Wolves staged one heck of a rally in which Swinbourne, Hancocks and Broadbent all missed the target, and Slater needed treatment for mild concussion. That it wasn't going to be Wolves' day was emphasised in the 63rd minute by the referee when, after Shorthouse had been blatantly felled by Reid, he awarded a bounce-up instead of a free-kick to Wolves, and to add insult to injury, the ball reached Duggie Reid, who stuck it away unceremoniously. And that was that.

This was another defeat for Wolves, their first away from home since 26 August, this time on a ground where they hadn't lost since 1949. Pompey's second goal knocked the stuffing out of Wolves and they never recovered. They weren't brilliant, and certainly missed Wilshaw, but they surely did enough to have at least shared the points; perhaps with hindsight, the decision to rest Pritchard was wrong. Since the win at Tottenham on 5 December, Wolves had now lost 5 out of their last 8 games, including the Cup-tie with Birmingham. The boys needed to get the wheels firmly back on the wagon if we were to beat Albion to the title.

Albion increased their lead over Wolves to 2 points with a 0-0 draw against Burnley. Wolves needed to do something dramatic – and they did. But first, a long trip beckoned.

30 January 1954 was FA Cup fourth round day, and Wolves travelled to the north of Scotland to play a friendly against Aberdeen at Pittodrie Park. In the wake of the success of the friendly against

---

**Portsmouth 2**                         **Wolves 0**

*Dickinson (8)*

*Reid (63)*

Norman Deeley, Wolves.

Celtic, the Aberdeen directors were keen to be invited to play a return game under the Molineux floodlights. It snowed an hour before kick-off and must have been freezing cold; a not-so-bonnie Scotland that was sure. Wolves lost 5-3, their goals coming from Taylor, Flowers and Broadbent.

In the Cup, Albion beat Rotherham United 4-0 to ease into round five with two goals from Johnny Nicholls, plus one each from Ronnie Allen and Reg 'Paddy' Ryan.

---

**Portsmouth:** Platt; Wilson, Mansell; Phillips, Rutter, Dickinson; Harris, Gordon, Reid, Barnard, Henderson.
**Wolves:** Williams; Short, Wright; W.J. Slater, Shorthouse, Flowers; Hancocks, Deeley, Swinbourne, Broadbent, Mullen

# Wolves v. Blackpool Town

Football League Division One at Molineux
Date: Saturday 6 February 1954                    Attendance: 27,795

It was a severely under-strength Blackpool that were next up at Molineux. The absence of Stanley Matthews always meant that the crowd would be much lower, always providing, of course, that this bad news had been communicated to the public; as was so often the case, it hadn't. Incidentally, when Stan played at Molineux, and most probably every other English football ground, a sizeable crowd would assemble along the right wing on each side of the pitch a good hour before kick-off in order to guarantee a close-up view of the maestro at work.

Also missing from the Blackpool line-up would be England duo centre half Harry Johnston and ace striker Stan Mortenson. Facing the visitors on this bitterly cold afternoon was an almost full-strength Wolves line-up, only Broadbent missing, his place being taken by Ron Flowers.

The Seasiders' reserves put up a spirited fight on the snow-covered surface, on which, rather surprisingly, the ball ran pretty true, often resorting to a robust and bruising kind of style in their efforts to contain Wolves' stars. And Wolves had a lot of stars on show that day. However, the brightest of them was Roy Swinbourne, who finally managed to recapture his sparkling form of earlier in the season, scoring his first hat-trick of the campaign. Surprisingly, both sets of players adjusted well to the slippery conditions to the extent that they made it seem easy to keep their feet.

As expected, Wolves hammered away relentlessly at the visitors' defence in which Farm had to be alert on any number of occasions to keep the slate clean. Johnny Hancocks opened Wolves' account in the 17th minute to set them back on the road to recovery with the only goal of the first half. With this goal, Johnny equalled his previous best goalscoring record by moving onto 19 goals for the season to date, matching his previous best from the season before. Taking a lovely pass from Bill Slater in his stride, the winger cut inside before sending the ball left to Jimmy Mullen. Johnny controlled the return pass and played it to Swinbourne, who wrong-footed the Blackpool defence by back-heeling the ball into Hancocks' path for Wolves' number seven to power in a ferocious shot that whizzed past George Farm in the Blackpool goal.

Then came the Roy Swinbourne show. Roy's first came in the 54th minute after good work and an exquisite pass from Ron Flowers. Then, in the 70th minute, Wolves were stung by a neat goal from centre forward Len Stephenson. The young number nine was first to a bouncing through-ball before Bill Shorthouse could react to close him down. With 6 minutes remaining, Roy Swinbourne got his second and Wolves' third, somewhat bizarrely. Jimmy Mullen whipped in a tremendous shot that might have gone wide; the ball cannoning into the net off the falling Swinbourne, who had somehow managed to get his foot to the ball. A minute later Swinbourne scored the goal of the

---

**Wolves 4**                                      **Blackpool 1**
*Hancocks (17)*                                   *Stephenson (70)*
*Swinbourne 3 (54, 84 and 85)*

# WOLVES v. BLACKPOOL TOWN

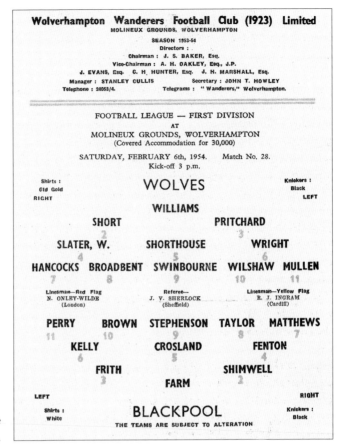

Wolverhampton Wanderers Football Club (1923) Limited
MOLINEUX GROUNDS, WOLVERHAMPTON

SEASON 1953-54

Directors :

Chairman : J. S. BAKER, Esq.

Vice-Chairman : A. H. OAKLEY, Esq., J.P.

J. EVANS, Esq.    C. H. HUNTER, Esq.    J. H. MARSHALL, Esq.

Manager : STANLEY CULLIS        Secretary : JOHN T. HOWLEY

Telephone : 24053/4.        Telegrams : " Wanderers," Wolverhampton.

FOOTBALL LEAGUE — FIRST DIVISION
AT
MOLINEUX GROUNDS, WOLVERHAMPTON
(Covered Accommodation for 30,000)

SATURDAY, FEBRUARY 6th, 1954.    Match No. 28.
Kick-off 3 p.m.

Shirts :    Knickers :
Old Gold    Black
RIGHT    WOLVES    LEFT

WILLIAMS

SHORT        PRITCHARD
2        3

SLATER, W.    SHORTHOUSE    WRIGHT
4        5        6

HANCOCKS  BROADBENT  SWINBOURNE  WILSHAW  MULLEN
7        8        9        10        11

Linesman—Red Flag        Referee—        Linesman—Yellow Flag
N. ONLEY-WILDE        J. V. SHERLOCK        R. J. INGRAM
(London)        (Sheffield)        (Cardiff)

PERRY      BROWN    STEPHENSON    TAYLOR    MATTHEWS
11        10        9        8        7

KELLY        CROSLAND        FENTON
6        5        4

FRITH        SHIMWELL
3        2

FARM

LEFT        RIGHT

Shirts :    Knickers :
White    BLACKPOOL    Black

THE TEAMS ARE SUBJECT TO ALTERATION

Team page – programme
Wolves v. Blackpool.

game. Before Farm could move, Wolves' big number nine took the ball to his left before unleashing an unstoppable left-foot shot that had the Blackpool net bulging.

Despite the emphatic scoreline, it hadn't been all one-way traffic by any means. Bert Williams had to be at his most alert to keep out a couple of good efforts from the Blackpool youngsters, the pick of whom was Brown. With an aggressive edge to his scheming, he looked dangerous whenever he had the ball. But in the end Wolves were worthy winners.

This win wasn't enough to take Wolves back to the top of the table, as Albion's better goal average would have kept them there even if they had lost; they didn't anyway, drawing 1-1 with Charlton at the Valley, Allen netting again. Still 1 point in it: WBA 42 points, Wolves 41.

**Wolves:** Williams; Short, Pritchard; W.J. Slater, Shorthouse, Wright; Hancocks, Flowers, Swinbourne, Wilshaw, Mullen

**Blackpool:** Farm; Shimwell, Frith; Fenton, Crosland, Kelly; Harris, Mudie, Stephenson, Brown, Perry

# CHELSEA V. WOLVES

**Football League Division One at Stamford Bridge**

**Date:** Saturday 13 February 1954          **Attendance:** 60,276

---

Why can't Wolves be consistent? That was the question on most fans' lips following this six-goal thriller. A staggering crowd of over 60,000 turned up to see the team that had beaten Chelsea 8-1 at Molineux in September – I guess most of them were gagging for revenge. The crowd didn't have to wait long for the fun to start; less than a minute in fact.

On 50 seconds, England centre forward Roy Bentley controlled a lovely pass from Armstrong and smacked the ball home to put Wolves immediately on the back foot. With the game only 7 minutes old, a midfield collision involving three players left Wolves' centre half Bill Shorthouse writhing in pain with a nasty rib injury. After initial treatment at the scene, Bill had to leave the field, which is where he stayed for a full 18 minutes before he was able to return to the fray. Billy Wright took over in the centre of Wolves' defence, and Ron Flowers moved to left-half. In the meantime, right-winger Eric Parsons claimed a second for Chelsea in the 19th minute against ten-man Wolves, his shot going in off a post. Bentley drifted out to the right wing and delivered a precise pass into the winger's run; Williams had no chance.

At this stage of the game Wolves were being completely outplayed, and what was worse, they were beginning to look beaten already. Shorthouse took up a position in Wolves' attack, but was obviously still in a state of some distress, unable to provide more than a nuisance value.

Just prior to the half-hour mark, Wolves regrouped and took the fight to Chelsea, forcing a corner which, in truth, Harris gave away needlessly. The ball came over and there was Roy Swinbourne shooting through a crowd of Chelsea defenders to grab a lifeline for Wolves. That's how it stayed until the interval.

The second period emphasised Wolves' shortage of manpower; however, in the face of some severe Chelsea pressure, they made a real fist of it. Bentley was causing all kinds of scary moments by constantly wandering out to the right, in doing so often dragging Wright out of position. This enabled Stubbs and McNichol to use the space down the middle to good effect. Despite this, Wolves held out until just past the hour, when McNichol's neat through-ball found Parsons on the right. His hard centre was met perfectly by Les Stubbs, who stabbed in the home side's third.

Wolves weren't done yet and came back at Chelsea with some vigour. In the 64th minute Dennis Wilshaw met a fiercely struck cross from Hancocks to bring the score back to 3-2. A lovely goal, almost a carbon copy of Chelsea's third; could Wolves draw level? Bill Shorthouse, now playing at centre forward, almost did it a few minutes later, but unfortunately for Wolves his flashing header was saved and the Pensioners breathed a sigh of relief.

The end of a mad 5 minutes was signalled in the 67th minute by Roy Bentley's second of the game. Armstrong sent in a long cross that Bentley headed home from two yards to make it 4-2 to Chelsea.

---

### Chelsea 4
*Bentley 2 (50 seconds and 67)*
*Parsons (19)*
*Stubbs (62)*

### Wolves 2
*Swinbourne (30)*
*Wilshaw (64)*

Action from Chelsea *v.* Wolves at Stamford Bridge. Bert Williams punches clear of Bentley and Stubbs of Chelsea.

There was no way back for Wolves. Their courageous performance probably deserved something from this game, but in the end Wanderers got nothing. Obviously the injury to Bill Shorthouse greatly affected their ability to produce a performance in the mould of the one seen against Blackpool.

Sadly for Wolves' fans, Albion came back from a 2-0 deficit to beat Sheffield Wednesday 4-2, and thus stretch their lead over Wolves to 3 points. Their goals came from Nicholls, Rickaby and Ryan, plus an own goal by Butler.

|        | PLD | W  | D | L | F  | A  | PTS |
|--------|-----|----|---|---|----|----|-----|
| Albion | 30  | 19 | 6 | 5 | 75 | 39 | 44  |
| **Wolves** | **30** | **18** | **5** | **7** | **70** | **45** | **41** |

Round five of the FA Cup was to be played on the following Saturday, and Albion were fortunate to have received the benefit of a home draw against Newcastle United. Wolves would entertain underachieving Sheffield United at Molineux in the League.

In mid-February 1954, Bill Slater decided to change his playing status from amateur to semi-professional. This was around the time that Bill had accepted a post as lecturer at Birmingham University, and he was keen to retain his amateur status, sometimes finding it difficult to train with the Wolves' first-team squad. Bill had played in Blackpool's losing team against Newcastle United in the 1951 FA Cup final, and had subsequently played several times for Brentford, before signing for Wolves in August 1952, thus joining another former Brentford player at the club, Peter Broadbent. His first game as a professional would prove to be memorable.

---

**Chelsea:** Thompson; Harris, Willemse; Armstrong, Greenwood, Saunders (D); Parsons, McNichol, Bentley, Stubbs, Blunstone

**Wolves:** Williams; Short, Pritchard; W.J. Slater, Shorthouse, Wright; Hancocks, Flowers, Swinbourne, Wilshaw, Mullen

# WOLVES v. SHEFFIELD UNITED

Fottball League Division One at Molineux
Date: Saturday 20 February 1954                    Attendance: 27,832

Bill Slater was given a fine reception by the fans, who all prayed that their team could return to winning ways as well as receiving a little bit of the luck that had recently appeared to desert them. Sheffield United were lambs prime for the slaughter: they languished at the bottom end of the table, hoping that Wolves would show them some mercy; they didn't. This was a Molineux day to remember as a rampant Wolves swept aside United's puny defence to thump in six goals. At last the shooting boots were on and well aimed.

Eddie Stuart took over at right-back for his first game of the season, having made his first-team debut two seasons earlier at centre forward against the Baggies at The Hawthorns. Stuart had been struck down by a mystery illness in 1952 that kept him out of the first-eleven picture for a long period. Billy Wright continued at centre half in the absence of the injured Bill Shorthouse, who hadn't recovered from his nasty rib injury at Chelsea. Ron Flowers kept the number 6 shirt. Johnny Hancocks was on the brink of setting a new record for the number of goals scored by a winger in one season; he was determined to grab the goal that would break his own record, set in the previous season.

The new line-up looked good and made their opponents from Yorkshire appear even more inferior than they were, although the accuracy of Hancocks' shooting left a lot to be desired. First, Wilshaw set him up with a great scoring opportunity that the right-winger blazed high and wide, before repeating the feat from a lovely Swinbourne pass that saw him miss from only a yard or so from the right-hand goalpost; it looked impossible to put the ball over from such close range.

Wolves pressed and pressed, but as it turned out, it took them half an hour to break through the visitor' dogged defence. The fun was finally begun by Roy Swinbourne who, on 33 minutes, following Stuart's excellent long pass, deliberately deflected a ferocious effort from Hancocks past the unfortunate Ted Burgin in the Blades' goal, Swinbourne's 20th of the season.

Shortly after this, United's ace schemer Hagan took a bad knock, which left him virtually unable to influence the game. And then a minute before half-time, it was again a long raking pass from Stuart to Hancocks that set up Swinbourne's and Wolves' second, to send the teams in at 2-0. The Wolves' centre forward collected Hancocks' pass and muscled aside Johnson to beat Burgin with a low shot for his 21st of the campaign.

The second half began and ended in whirlwind fashion. A minute after the restart, Wilshaw crossed and Johnny Hancocks, running towards goal, sent in a powerful header that came back to him off Burgin's hands for the diminutive winger to notch his 20th goal of the season with a neat shot, so breaking his previous best goal-scoring record. From now on every goal he scored would

---

**Wolves 6**
  Swinbourne 2 (33 and 44),
  Hancocks 2 (46 and 56), Broadbent (84),
  Wilshaw (89)

**Sheffield United 1**
  Cross (86)

set a new record. Later in the game, the winger was guilty of his second miss-of-the-match when he again skied the ball high into the Cowshed; he really should have scored.

Then it was Peter Broadbent's turn to get into the scoring act with a nice goal that was subsequently ruled out for offside. A few minutes later, Hancocks almost broke the net with another explosive effort for his 21st. Then came the coup de grâce, administered by slick Wolves in a thrilling 6-minute finale. In the 84th minute, Wilshaw sent Broadbent away for the inventive inside right to score a legitimate goal to make it five.

Understandably, Wolves eased their feet off the gas a little, resulting in Sheffield United producing a couple of effective attacks. Cross and Hawksworth had already missed a couple of reasonable chances when, with 4 minutes remaining, centre forward Jack Cross went one better by scoring a consolation goal for the visitors. In a case of 'anything you can do', Dennis Wilshaw whipped in a great last-minute shot from 25 yards, his 21st of the season, to wrap it up at 6-1. What a feat! Three of Wolves' attack had each scored 21 goals.

Having three players who had each scored 21 goals was a fantastic feat, and a tribute to Wolves, and Cullis' policy of all-out attack.

The emphatic win over United brought Wolves back to 1 point behind Albion, who had eased into round four of the Cup with a Ronnie Allen hat-trick, his 4th of the season, enabling them to beat Newcastle 3-2 in a tough Cup-tie at The Hawthorns. Wolves' win couldn't get them back to the top of the League, even with Albion playing in the Cup.

One of the most disappointing aspects of the season was that so many fans were staying away from Molineux. Few people could understand exactly why this was. There was usually plenty of excitement, thrills and spills in abundance, plus goals galore.

On the following Wednesday, Albion travelled to Ayresome Park and earned a 1-1 draw with Middlesbrough, Allen again getting their goal, to increase their lead at the top to 2 points.

|  | PLD | W | D | L | F | A | PTS |
|---|---|---|---|---|---|---|---|
| Albion | 31 | 19 | 7 | 5 | 76 | 40 | 45 |
| **Wolves** | 31 | 19 | 5 | 7 | 76 | 46 | 43 |

**Wolves:** Williams; Stuart, Pritchard; Slater, Wright, Flowers; Hancocks, Broadbent, Swinbourne, Wilshaw, Mullen

**Sheffield United:** Burgin; Coldwell, Shaw (G); Shaw (J), Johnson, Rawson; Ringstead, Hagan, Cross, Hawksworth, Grainger

# WOLVES V. NEWCASTLE UNITED

**Football League Division One at Molineux**

**Date:** Saturday 27 February 1954　　　　　**Attendance:** 38,592

---

Wolves set about the task of putting the Geordies firmly in their place, with the happy memory of the six-goal thrashing handed out to Sheffield United a week earlier still fresh in their minds; they were like an express train, powerful and fast. It might have been a bitterly cold February afternoon, but the good-sized crowd were soon able to warm their hands in applause for their heroes.

In the 4th minute, Bert Williams collected a loose ball, looked up and put Wolves on the attack with a glorious throw to Johnny Hancocks. The winger nudged the ball into the path of Peter Broadbent near the centre circle, and off went Pete on a mazy run. Out came centre half Brennan and the Newcastle goalkeeper Ronnie Simpson, both colliding with the Wolves number eight. Accident or deliberate? Either way, the referee waved play on. Broadbent was first to recover, sizing up the situation in an instant, quickly latching on to the ball before threading it into the visitors' net; fabulous stuff.

Newcastle weren't about to lie down, and came back at Wolves with some vigour, threatening to equalise through a couple of good efforts by England international inside forward Ivor Broadis, who earlier in the season had played for Manchester City against Wolves. 'Wor' Jackie Milburn also went close for the visitors. Wisps of snow began to fall to bring a Christmassy feel to the proceedings.

On 20 minutes, the ever-stylish Broadbent cleverly stepped over the ball and there was Dennis Wilshaw to smack the ball home with a rising shot to give Wolves a well-deserved 2-0 lead. Less than 10 minutes later, Bill Slater was hurt in a nasty collision. Fortunately he was able to continue after a generous application of the cold sponge by trainer Joe Gardiner.

A second Wolves player was injured before the referee had whistled for the break. Roy Swinbourne fell awkwardly following a heavy Geordie challenge; he was visibly stunned by the collision, and took a little time to get to his feet. When he did, it was obvious that he was still badly shaken. Hopefully the half-time interval would give him time to recover. A bit more snow had the crowd huddling together for warmth, many unwilling to risk the queue for a hot Bovril.

When the teams emerged for the second half, it was obvious that Swinbourne was still in a great deal of distress. That he carried on was a tribute to both his bravery and his loyalty to the team and the manager; he managed one effort that produced a great one-handed tip over from Simpson, but after a while, all Roy could do was hobble along on the wing. Wolves were now virtually playing with ten men, and starting to allow Newcastle to capitalise upon their numerical superiority.

The snow that by now was falling heavily must have obscured Wolves' defenders' vision as, 10 minutes before the end following an excellent Newcastle move that saw Brennan link up well with his attack, the talented Broadis set up a good chance for Jackie Milburn. The Geordie folk hero smacked in a left-foot shot from a tight angle that this time didn't miss. After witnessing a display of

---

**Wolves 3**　　　　　　　　　　　　**Newcastle United 2**

　*Broadbent (4)*　　　　　　　　　　　*Milburn (80)*

　*Wilshaw (20)*　　　　　　　　　　　*Broadis (85)*

　*Slater (86)*

# WOLVES v. NEWCASTLE UNITED

Bill Slater, Wolverhampton Wanderers.

dogged defending by Wolves, the faithful fully expected the lads to hold out for a 2-1 win, and for a long time it looked as though they would do it, but 5 minutes before the end the ball was thumped into Wolves' area by McMichael. After Williams had parried his first shot, Broadis managed to force the ball over the line to make it 2-2.

Not the worst result considering all the circumstances, thought many of the crowd who now began to trudge from the terraces, hoping to be first in the queue for their bus home. Wanderers had other ideas and stormed back at the Geordies, bombarding their defence from both wings. Miraculously, Wolves scored. Hancocks thundered over an explosive corner, at which brave Bill Slater thrust his head. The ball rocketed into the net and Bill was knocked out cold. This was Bill's second goal of the season and his first as a professional. Would the Geordies manage to come back again and rob Wolves of a precious point? Most of the crowd hoped not. With almost the last kick of the game Jimmy Mullen thought he'd made certain, but his firecracker of a shot crashed against a post, but it didn't matter because Wolves had won 3-2. Wolves' third home win in a row was a fabulous victory and one that was thoroughly deserved. Oh, and yes, Bill Slater recovered, but most probably with a sizeable headache.

Ryan and Nicholls scored to cement Albion's fine 2-0 win at high-flying Huddersfield Town, bringing their unbeaten run to 9 matches. This meant that, with 10 games left, there was no change at the top; Albion with 47 points, 2 ahead of Wolves' 45. But who would hold their nerve best on the run-in?

So, into mad March and next up for Wolves was Manchester United, who were also hovering just below the leaders.

---

**Wolves:** Williams; Stuart, Shorthouse; Slater, Wright, Flowers; Hancocks, Broadbent, Swinbourne, Wilshaw, Mullen

**Newcastle United:** Simpson; Cowell, McMichael; Stokoe, Brennan, Casey; Foulkes, Broadis, Milburn, Hannah, Mitchell

# Manchester United v. Wolves

**Football League Division One at Old Trafford**

**Date:** Saturday 6 March 1954          **Attendance:** 38,930

---

The result of this game hinged on one moment of controversy involving, surprise, surprise, a dodgy decision by the match officials that allowed an 86th-minute offside goal by United to stand. However, let's start at the beginning.

This match was a cracker from kick-off to full-time, packed with the kind of thrills and spills normally reserved for a cup tie, and in which another day might have seen both teams score a hatful. Playing against the 'Busby Babes', Wolves had a couple of 'babes' of their own on show. Aside from the football, this game was notable as it marked the debut in the United youth team of a sixteen-year-old from Dudley by the name of Duncan Edwards. In an experimental move, with Swinbourne still injured, Wolves pushed young Ron Flowers up front to lead the attack, his left-half berth being filled by nineteen-and-a-half-year-old debutant Eddie Clamp. Both youngsters ran themselves into the ground.

Johnny Berry for United, ably assisted by the always tricky Dennis Viollet, was always a threat, although it was Flowers who could have made a name for himself with a couple of fine efforts. One was well saved by Ray Wood, the other he skied over the bar from six yards. For some reason, Stan Cullis' team had set out their stall to play an uncharacteristic style involving offside tactics, which, by the way, worked pretty well. At least it had until the incident involving the suggestion of officials' myopia as the game drew to a close.

Having described Wolves' defensive approach, on the offensive side of the coin the lads from Wolverhampton created enough chances to have won the game, a claim that would no doubt also be made by United fans. Jimmy Mullen certainly had the beating of big Bill Foulkes, but for some unfathomable reason he was starved of the ball for long periods. Wanderers' midfielders were in great form, sending through a steam of dangerous passes that were completely wasted. Hancocks and Wilshaw missed with a couple of efforts that really should have been despatched into the United net. Broadbent and Flowers were also guilty of squandering good opportunities in this full-bloodied and rousing match. The game was so full of incident that it was hard to believe that the score was 0-0 until the 86th minute. That's when disaster struck for Wolves in the form of a linesman: Berry was clearly at least 2 yards offside when the ball was pushed through to him.

Wolves' defenders stopped, the linesman raised his flag and the referee's whistle approached his lips. Amazingly, the linesman's elasticated flag suddenly went down before the ref could blow. A static Bert Williams watched in horror as the United winger slammed a fierce shot into Wolves' net, and it was all over. Every Wolves protest fell on deaf eyes, as Wanderers were forced to accept a cruel defeat when a draw would have been a much fairer result.

---

**Manchester United 1**                    **Wolves 0**

*Berry (86)*

88

# Manchester United v. Wolves

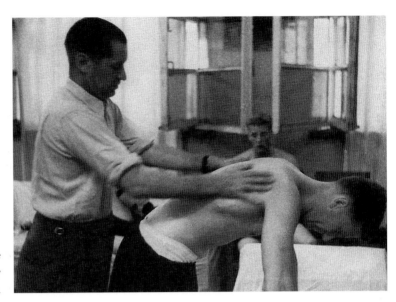

Wolves trainer Joe Gardiner massages Roy Swinbourne's back.

Berry had signalled his quality in the 25th minute when he went round Bill Shorthouse as if he wasn't there only to shoot into the side-netting with only Bert Williams to beat. Wolves' heads didn't drop, and attack after attack was launched at the Reds' backline. Unfortunately, each ended in disappointment as the Manchester United defence resolutely defied everything that was thrown at them. There just wasn't enough time left to grab the equaliser. Sadly, young Eddie Clamp got a bit of stick despite doing okay against the talented ex-Brummie Johnny Berry. And by and large, Billy Wright managed to keep England centre forward Tommy Taylor fairly quiet. In fact, most of the team played well, although Bill Slater did have a bit of an off day when compared to the high standards that he had set in previous games.

Fortunately for Wolves, Albion could only manage a 2-2 draw at home to Sheffield United, Nicholls and Lee on target, so their lead was still only 3 points.

Four days later, Wolves' fans were treated to the third friendly game under the Molineux floodlights; it had been a wait of six months since the Celtic game. This one would also prove to be memorable as the faithful were introduced to a completely different style of football: the right-back acting as a deep centre half, the right-half at right-back, the centre half roving and the centre forward playing deep to draw the opposing defence – a bit confusing in those days. Today, we might consider it a bit old-fashioned compared to the almost innumerable playing systems we are used to: 4-4-2, 4-2-4, 3-5-2, 4-3-3, the Christmas tree, the diamond, the hokey-cokey 2000! Actually, this one seems pretty simple; but in any case this was Argentinian football, and it was coming to Molineux.

**Manchester United:** Wood; Foulkes, Byrne; Whitefoot, Chilton, Edwards; Berry, Blanchflower, Taylor, Viollet, Rowley

**Wolves:** Williams; Stuart, Shorthouse; Slater, Wright, Clamp; Hancocks, Broadbent, Flowers, Wilshaw, Mullen

# WOLVES V. RACING CLUB OF BUENOS AIRES

**Floodlit Friendly at Molineux**

**Date:** Wednesday 10 March 1954          **Attendance:** 37,122

On Wednesday 10 March 1954, Wolves took on the pride of Argentina – Racing Club of Buenos Aires, a team noted for their delightful brand of football, and for their singing of the club anthem, 'The Cancione de America' (Song of America) on the way to a match.

By the time they reached Molineux, the Argentinians had already played matches in Rome, Zagreb, Belgrade, Valencia, Bilbao, Madrid and Brussels. Following their game with Wolves, Racing were scheduled to round off the British leg of their tour against Chelsea and West Ham before playing the final game of their European tour in Paris.

Interestingly, in a preview of the game, one newspaper described the visitors as 'those gay caballeros from Racing Club'. Another thing I remember about this match was the rumour that the Racing Club trainer reputedly carried a bottle of large red-meat vitamin pills in his bag. Apparently these were used at half-time to supplement or top-up the energy levels of his players. My mate told me this – I don't know if it was true or if he was taking the mickey, but he was older than me (13), so it must have been true. Anyway, these guys from the Argentine used to perform a series of dainty balletic twirls and contortions as their warm-up, which incidentally failed to confuse the mighty Wolves, who that night played powerful and purposeful quick-fire football that didn't disappoint any of the crowd and let them run out easy winners 3-1.

The South Americans themselves weren't completely without merit. They played an immaculate short-passing game involving constant positional interchanges, and were obviously specialists in ball control. Coupled with great heading ability, their football was impressive, and surprisingly their sportsmanship was first class. Mind you, if the 'pill story' was true, the pills weren't very effective because the Argentinians certainly didn't seem to have much beef!

Leading Wolves' attack that night and deputising for the injured Roy Swinbourne was debutant Doug Taylor. It was Doug who scored Wolves' opening goal after 16 minutes when he tapped in a downward header from Dennis Wilshaw. We all went crackers with joy, but were quickly silenced when, less than a minute later, the Argentinians drew level, turning our cheers to tears. Veteran international Mendez slipped the ball through the middle for Pizzuti to flash it into the net, a fine goal of speed and precision. On the hour, Norman Deeley playing at left-half hit a screaming 25-yarder to make it 2-1.

Just 11 minutes later, Jimmy Mullen sealed it for Wolves with a smart cross-shot; now it was cheers of joy as the referee blew for full-time. All too frequently the Racing Club forwards ran into offside positions, consequently causing the referee to have to keep stopping the game. Perhaps it was the skill of Wolves' defenders that confused them – who knows? Wolves won, so who cared?

---

**Wolves 3**                               **Racing Club of Buenos Aires 1**
*Taylor (16)*                                  *Pizzuti (17)*
*Deeley (60)*
*Mullen (71)*

# WOLVES v. RACING CLUB OF BUENOS AIRES

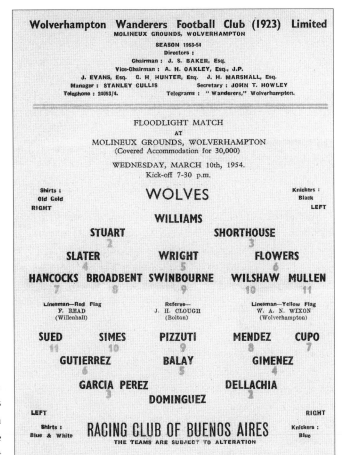

**Wolverhampton Wanderers Football Club (1923) Limited**
MOLINEUX GROUNDS, WOLVERHAMPTON
SEASON 1953-54
Directors :
Chairman : J. S. BAKER, Esq.
Vice-Chairman : A. H. OAKLEY, Esq., J.P.
J. EVANS, Esq.    C. H. HUNTER, Esq.    J. H. MARSHALL, Esq.
Manager : STANLEY CULLIS        Secretary : JOHN T. HOWLEY
Telephone : 24053/4.        Telegrams : " Wanderers," Wolverhampton.

FLOODLIGHT MATCH
AT
MOLINEUX GROUNDS, WOLVERHAMPTON
(Covered Accommodation for 30,000)
WEDNESDAY, MARCH 10th, 1954.
Kick-off 7-30 p.m.

Shirts :          **WOLVES**          Knickers :
Old Gold                              Black
RIGHT                                  LEFT

WILLIAMS

STUART        SHORTHOUSE
2                 3

SLATER    WRIGHT    FLOWERS
4          5          6

HANCOCKS BROADBENT SWINBOURNE WILSHAW MULLEN
7          8          9         10      11

Linesman—Red Flag    Referee—        Linesman—Yellow Flag
F. READ          J. H. CLOUGH        W. A. N. WIXON
(Willenhall)        (Bolton)          (Wolverhampton)

SUED    SIMES    PIZZUTI    MENDEZ    CUPO
11      10         9          8        7

GUTIERREZ    BALAY    GIMENEZ
6             5          4

GARCIA PEREZ    DELLACHIA
3               2

DOMINGUEZ
1

LEFT                                              RIGHT

Shirts :    **RACING CLUB OF BUENOS AIRES**    Knickers :
Blue & White    THE TEAMS ARE SUBJECT TO ALTERATION    Blue

Team page – programme Wolves v. Racing Club of Buenos Aires. As you can see, there were quite a number of changes made to the line-up on the night

The following weekend was strange because Wolves had no game to play. It was sixth-round Saturday and their game with Bolton Wanderers had been postponed because of the other Wanderers' continued involvement in the FA Cup. Mind you, as the Baggies were also still in the Cup, at least Wolves wouldn't lose any further ground on them. Albion were to play Tottenham Hotspur at The Hawthorns on 13 March, running out 3-0 winners in a one-sided game, courtesy of two goals from Johnny Nicholls and one from Ray Barlow, to reach the FA Cup semi-finals.

Four days later, on 17 March, Albion were well and truly walloped 5-0 by Chelsea to give Wolves a little hope in the title race. They were 3 points behind, and now with a game in hand, but first they faced one of the other FA Cup semi-finalists.

**Wolves:** Williams; Stuart, Shorthouse; Slater, Wright, Deeley; Hancocks, Broadbent, Taylor, Wilshaw, Mullen
**Racing Club of Buenos Aires:** Dominguez; Dellachia, Fernandez; Gimenez, Balay, Alvarez; Cupo, Mendez, Pizzuti, Simes, Sued

# PRESTON NORTH END v. WOLVES

Football League Division One at Deepdale
Date: Saturday 20 March 1954          Attendance: 28,857

In a reversal of fortune, Wolves came away from this hard-fought game against Preston with all of the points, the game for all intents and purposes having looked like a solid-gold draw until the 80th minute. Stan Cullis changed the line-up once again. Out went Flowers and Clamp, and in at left-half came another of Wolves' youngsters, Norman Deeley, who had played so well against the Argentinians. Deeley was still only twenty and making his fourth first-team appearance. Roy Swinbourne had regained full fitness and returned to lead the attack, with the reliable Les Smith deputising for Jimmy Mullen on the left wing.

Wolves were bolstered by the news that ace winger Tom Finney wouldn't be playing, nor would Wayman or Forbes. Future Wolves manager, joker Tommy Docherty, would be at right half. Wolves' line-up meant they could return to their 'power-play' style of bombardment, against which Thompson, the Preston goalkeeper, often stood defiantly alone to keep baying Wolves out. Thompson demonstrated this as early as the 1st minute, when he saved a thunderous shot from Hancocks. It could have been goals galore as shot after shot was saved or missed at both ends, but the miss of the game came from Johnny Hancocks. Man of the match Les Smith pulled the ball across the area, only for the little winger to completely fluff his shot from 6 yards out, and this after Roy Swinbourne had taken first turn to miss the ball totally.

As the game moved into its final phase, it looked as though both teams had resigned themselves to a draw. However, it was the visitors from Wolverhampton that were finishing the stronger, and eventually Wolves got the goal they so desperately desired. Once again, it was Les Smith the provider, his clever 80th-minute pass finding Dennis Wilshaw in space.

Wolves' number ten controlled the ball and sent in a hopeful 25-yard long-range shot that somehow deceived Thompson before rebounding into the net from his far post. Game, set and match? No, actually. Preston's youthful team hit back with a string of attacks that had all those connected with Wolves gnawing at their fists. Thankfully, twice in the dying minutes inside left Jones contrived to miss when maybe he should have done better.

The referee blew for time and a much-relieved Wolves left the field. Wanderers just about deserved this narrow victory, Billy Wright once again solid at centre half, without ever reaching the heights of some previous performances. Nevertheless, as they say in football, it's the mark of a good team that they can still pick up the points when not playing well.

Albion recovered their League form with a 2-1 home win against Blackpool, the goals coming from Allen and Ryan. So again nothing changed at the top of the League. Albion 50 points, Wolves 47.

---

**Preston 0**                    **Wolves 1**
                                 *Wilshaw (80)*

Tom Finney, Preston North End.

Wolves now had a chance to close the gap, or even go above their rivals, because of the two League fixtures they were about to play. Albion's next game would be the FA Cup semi-final.

---

**Preston North End:** Thompson; Cunningham, Walton; Docherty, Marston, Dunn; Campbell, Baxter, Hatsell, Jones, Morrison

**Wolves:** Williams; Stuart, Shorthouse; Slater, Wright, Deeley; Hancocks, Broadbent, Swinbourne, Wilshaw, Smith

# WOLVES V. BOLTON WANDERERS

**Football League Division One at Molineux**

**Date:** Wednesday 24 March 1954                    **Attendance:** 19,617

---

Dennis Wilshaw was unable to get time off from his day job as schoolmaster in time to get to this late afternoon game. So for this one, Stan Cullis brought in Eddie Clamp at inside left to partner Les Smith, with Norman Deeley retaining his place at left half. Pretty much a reserve left side.

Spearheading a first-class Bolton attack was England's centre forward, the 'Lion of Vienna', Nat Lofthouse. An anticipated low turnout of below 20,000 on this cold, but otherwise dry afternoon, was treated to an absorbing game in which, once again, Wolves' young cubs acquitted themselves well.

Roy Swinbourne looked hungry for goals and skimmed the bar with a fierce drive as early as the first minute. Then, at the other end Hassall also screamed one over. Wolves surged back and a high bouncing ball from young Clamp clearly hit the hand of Banks. Penalty? No, the referee waved play on.

Wolves continued to have the better of the early exchanges, and then the unthinkable happened when Nat Lofthouse opened the scoring for the Trotters in the 10th minute. The England number nine chased a long clearance from Barrass, racing past Billy Wright almost as though he was standing still. Williams started to advance out of his goal, but for some reason hesitated before retreating a step or two, allowing Nat to slip the ball past him.

One minute later, he did it again, but this time Stuart managed to get across to deflect his shot for a corner. Back came Wolves and, just after the quarter-of-an-hour mark, Swinbourne whipped in a low cross-cum-shot from the left, which was blocked but not cleared. Hancocks took a swipe at the ball but miscued, enabling Bell to put it out for a corner.

Wolves, composure restored, were now moving quite smoothly, probing for the equaliser. Stuart sent Clamp through, but the young wing half's shot flew straight into the grateful arms of Hanson. Then Swinbourne again skimmed the bar, this time from 25 yards. A few minutes later, Hancocks won a corner, from which Smith hit the crossbar with a fierce cross-shot, before Clamp set up another chance that the winger put a foot wide from 25 yards.

Danger then threatened for the Trotters when Barrass brought down Swinbourne outside the box and Hancocks grabbed the ball and attempted to lob the ball over Hanson. However, the referee called for the kick to be taken again as the Bolton players were not 10 yards from the ball. Hancocks repeated his attempted lob, which was well saved by Hanson.

Just 3 minutes before the break, Peter Broadbent picked up the ball near the centre-circle, found some space and from fully 30 yards out, powered in a shot of such ferocity that it flew past goalkeeper Hanson before he could move. Surely one of the goals of the season. Half-time came and went, and a quick Bovril later, the crowd was ready for a thrilling second half. Unfortunately, it didn't turn out that way.

---

**Wolves 1**                                        **Bolton Wanderers 1**

*Broadbent (42)*                                    *Lofthouse (10)*

# WOLVES v. BOLTON WANDERERS

Nat Lofthouse, Bolton Wanderers.

The game was often a quite dull affair on an even duller day. If only the League had allowed the use of floodlights for League games – at least that would have brightened things up a bit. From the interval onwards the contest, if one could call it that, became something of a stalemate, the highlight being the top-draw duel between Billy Wright and Nat Lofthouse. Still, 1-1 wasn't the end of the world, although Wolves had sacrificed their game in hand and remained 2 points adrift of the Baggies. However, Wolves would have the chance to draw level with their closest rivals on the following Saturday when the Baggies were due to face Third-Division Port Vale in the semi-final of the FA Cup at Villa Park, centre forward Ronnie Allen facing his home-town club – the team he played for before joining the Albion.

It was a wasted chance for Wolves. Still, they now had another shot at the top spot.

|        | PLD | W  | D | L | F  | A  | PTS |
|--------|-----|----|---|---|----|----|-----|
| Albion | 35  | 21 | 8 | 6 | 82 | 48 | 50  |
| **Wolves** | **35** | **21** | **6** | **8** | **81** | **50** | **48** |

**Wolves:** Williams; Stuart, Shorthouse; Slater, Wright, Deeley; Hancocks, Broadbent, Swinbourne, Clamp, Smith

**Bolton Wanderers:** Hanson; Ball, Banks (T); Hennin, Barrass, Bell; Holden, Moir, Lofthouse, Hassall, Parry

# WOLVES V. MIDDLESBROUGH

**Football League Division One at Molineux**

**Date:** Saturday 27 March 1954          **Attendance:** 29,145

---

What a squandered opportunity this was! Middlesbrough were close to bottom of the League; and would eventually be relegated at the end of the season. Contrastingly, Wolves were flying high in second place. This was a fabulous chance to draw level with the leaders, on points if not on goal difference. They blew it big time, as relegation anxiety triumphed over Championship aspiration!

At times during this game, Wanderers played at a half-hearted tempo that smacked of complacency. It was as if they believed that they only had to turn up to beat the Wearsiders, their poor display a real disappointment to the fans. As we all know only too well, football ain't like that, is it? I was always taught that success is a marriage of talent and endeavour. Where was Cullis' motto, 'There is no substitute for hard work'? It was unbelievable!

For the visitors, the skilful inside forward Wilf Mannion was in inspirational form and was at the heart of almost every good move for Boro. In goal, they had the acrobatic excellence of goalkeeper Rolando Ugolini. Together with some opportunistic finishing, Middlesbrough had these two to thank for the points on this grey Wolverhampton day.

Mannion started things off in the 3rd minute with a lovely flick that put Billy Watkin in the clear. The speedy left-winger fired the visitors into the lead with a carefully placed shot that flashed well wide of Williams' right hand.

A flash in the pan it wasn't, and 9 minutes later centre forward Ken McPherson thumped home number two. The elegant Delapenha started this excellent move with an exquisite pass, sending Watkin racing away down the left before sliding the ball into McPherson's path. The big number 9 made no mistake. Confident Boro were now playing some beautiful football.

With half-time approaching fast, Boro were awarded a penalty when Billy Wright's tackle was somewhat harshly adjudged to have brought down Lawrie. Lindy Delapenha wasted no time in putting the ball past Williams.

3-0 at the break was the stuff of nightmares. Wolves' forwards had left their shooting boots at home. They just couldn't get it right in front of goal, and when they did manage to get a shot on target, Ugolini was equal to the challenge, pulling off a series of incredible saves from Wilshaw, Deeley and Hancocks.

I'm sure that some of the home fans were thinking long and hard about going home when, in the 73rd minute, they were perked up by Peter Broadbent, who showed the rest of his mates how to do it. In a 5-minute spell, the Wolves number eight scored two to bring a measure of hope back into Wolves' hearts. His first was a fierce low cross-shot that flew past Ugolini following a nice pass from Swinbourne, and his second was a header from Mullen's corner.

---

**Wolves 2**

*Broadbent 2 (73 and 78)*

**Middlesbrough 4**

*Watkin (3),*

*Delapenha (penalty) (43)*

*McPherson 2 (12 and 88)*

Unfortunately, the visitors performed this task a whole lot better than Wolves, the ultimate insult coming 2 minutes from time. Wright and McPherson leaped high to contest a high bouncing ball following Ugolini's long goal kick. Depressingly for Wolves, McPherson came out on top of this particular duel, grabbing his second to secure the match for Boro.

Isn't it just crackers how things turn out sometimes? Apart from a fighting revival late in the second half, Wolves were simply outplayed, never managing to recover from conceding 2 goals in the first 12 minutes

Wolves were still 2 points behind the Throstles, having played one game more; not good.

|  | PLD | W | D | L | F | A | PTS |
|---|---|---|---|---|---|---|---|
| Albion | 35 | 21 | 8 | 6 | 82 | 48 | 50 |
| **Wolves** | **36** | **21** | **6** | **9** | **83** | **54** | **48** |

At Villa Park in front of 68,221 screaming fans, West Bromwich Albion just about managed to beat Third Division (North) leaders Port Vale 2-1 with a goal from Jimmy Dudley, plus a Ronnie Allen penalty in the dying minutes. Vale were the first Third Division team to reach the semi-final since the war. They went on to win the Third Division (North) title by 11 clear points. The Baggies had won their way through to the FA Cup final at Wembley, scheduled to be played on Saturday 1 May 1954.

In the League, Albion and Wolves had now played the same number of games, 36, and scored the same number of goals, 83, and only 2 points separated them at the top. So, the stage was set for a nail-biting run-in. In the other FA Cup semi-final, Preston North End beat Sheffield Wednesday 2-0. Wolves' next game might just prove to be a little difficult – it being away to West Bromwich Albion.

Albion's great Cup run was causing a bit of a fixture pile-up. Now they faced another mid-week game, this one at Sunderland on Wednesday 31 March, and an infamously significant game it turned out to be. In a dramatic few minutes, Albion were brought down to earth with a couple of huge bumps of bad luck that must have had manager Vic Buckingham tearing out his hair. He had already lost his two star strikers, Allen and Nicholls, to England, and now in a cruel twist of fate, Albion's Wolverhampton-born goalkeeper Norman Heath was crippled in a collision with Sunderland and ex-Birmingham forward Ted Purdon; a pure accident. Heath dived at Purdon's feet as he chased a cross from the right, Purdon in the process falling headlong over the Albion goalkeeper's head. It was believed that most likely Purdon's foot caught Heath's neck somewhere between the jaw bone and the shoulder blade, causing a concussion to the spinal nerve. The result was a temporary paralysis to both the keeper's legs. Sadly, Norman Heath never played football again. Ray Barlow took over in goal, but plucky ten-man Albion went down 2-1, Cox getting their goal in reply to Elliot and Purdon for Sunderland.

---

**Wolves:** Williams; Stuart, Shorthouse; Slater, Wright, Deeley; Hancocks, Broadbent, Swinbourne, Wilshaw, Mullen

**Middlesbrough:** Ugolini; Stonehouse, Corbett; Bell, Wicks, Harris; Lawrie, Mannion, McPherson, Delapenha, Watkin

# West Bromwich Albion v. Wolves

**Football League Division One at The Hawthorns**

**Date:** Saturday 3 April 1954        **Attendance:** 49,884

---

In addition to Heath, George Lee and Joe Kennedy were expected to be missing from Albion's line-up. Both had been injured in the bruising encounter at Sunderland. Also among the Baggies' walking wounded were Rickaby, Millard and Griffin, who were still being treated for knocks received in the FA Cup semi-final. All were thought to be doubtful for the game with Wolves. In the end, only Kennedy and Millard recovered sufficiently to play in the big one; a real 4-pointer.

Wolves couldn't afford to even contemplate losing this vital match. If Albion won, surely the title race would be all over bar the shouting. A daunting task considering Wanderers' track record at The Hawthorns. Apart from once in the 1940/41 War League Cup, they hadn't won there since the Second Division game on 10 November 1928, season 1928/29. In the intervening years, excluding the war years, Albion had won 9 times and drawn 3 times in the 12 seasons that the two clubs had competed in the same League.

Just to add a chunk of spice to the situation, the powers that be, the FA, had arranged for England to play Scotland in a Home International Championship/World Cup qualifier at Hampden Park, Glasgow, on this, the very same day as this real 'old-firm' Black Country derby! The bad news for Wolves was that Billy Wright and Jimmy Mullen had been selected to play for England. What could be worse?

Actually, the situation for Albion was worse because League top scorers Ronnie Allen and Johnny Nicholls had also been selected to play. So as well as missing the League game against Sunderland in mid-week, they would also miss this vital 4-pointer. This could never happen today. But as has already been explained, the FA had first call. The clubs could do nothing but accept the decision and get on with it.

On the playing front, Albion's luck seemed to have completely deserted them when news that Rickaby, Griffin and Lee would all be unavailable for this game. Five of the regular first eleven wouldn't play; Paddy Ryan would be the only recognised regular forward in their team.

On the left wing would be a young man by the name of Reg Cutler. Reg had only arrived home from Army duty on the Friday night before this match. Wolves' fans were to remember this lad when in 1957, playing for Bournemouth; he scored the goal that knocked us out of the FA Cup, and in the process helped shatter a goal post.

On this fateful day at The Hawthorns, the biggest game of the season as far as Wolves' and Albion fans were concerned was about to take place. With only six League games remaining, the outcome of this derby would surely determine the final resting place of the 1953/54 First Division Championship.

---

West Bromwich Albion 0          Wolves 1

*Swinbourne (58)*

# WEST BROMWICH ALBION v. WOLVES

The question on everyone's lips was which one of the severely handicapped teams would rise to the occasion. Most accepted that it was Albion's attack that had been the worst hit. They would be missing the joint strike force that had so far notched up 53 League goals between them. The next best was 7 each from inside forward Paddy Ryan and winger George Lee, whereas Wolves, apart from Mullen, were able to field a full first-team attack in which three players had scored more than 20 goals, Wilshaw 23, Hancocks and Swinbourne 21 each.

Almost 50,000 fans packed into The Hawthorns, tongues hanging out in anticipation of a classic encounter between two great teams. Unfortunately, a classic it wasn't – nowhere near one. Tension, fear of making a mistake and personnel changes certainly looked to affect both sides at various stages of the game, particularly Albion; the effect was to produce a bit of a dour affair to say the least.

Wolves' captain Bill Shorthouse, restored to his preferred centre half position in Wright's absence, gave as stout a display as ever, doing well to contain the lively Ray Barlow playing in the unaccustomed role of centre forward, and when Barlow took a nasty kick to the leg from Bill Shorthouse after only 8 minutes, his task was made even more simple.

Norman Heath, West Bromwich Albion.

# WEST BROMWICH ALBION v. WOLVES

Wolves' trainer Joe Gardiner (right) and future England international Ron Flowers.

Cutler had a couple of half-chances that wentbegging, and Ryan managed to fire in a couple of long-range shots, neither of which remotely threatened Williams' goal.

In Wolves' midfield, Peter Broadbent's play was superb, moving the ball around with speed and precision, setting up a number of chances for his fellow forwards that Albion's reserve goalkeeper Jimmy Sanders proved equal to.

At the other end, Bert Williams was having a fairly comfortable afternoon, and with Bill Slater and Eddie Stuart in a rich vein of form, things were looking good for the Wanderers.

The crowd weren't being overly treated excitement-wise, courtesy of a solid display from Kennedy and Dudley. Sanders was the recipient of good fortune after having been drawn out of position by Swinbourne, whose effort was cleared off the line by Millard who had raced back to cover. The Baggies' skipper did it again in the second half when he bravely headed away Hancocks' shot before it could cross the line. Both Swinbourne and Hancocks should have scored during this spell, and Wilshaw uncharacteristically missed a couple of reasonable chances. 0-0 at half-time was somewhat flattering to the Throstles.

The second half continued with more of the same, Wolves attacking and Albion defending doggedly until the 58th minute, when a moment of fantastic skill sent the Wolves' portion of the crowd crackers with joy. It was Roy Swinbourne, who had been in his second goal-drought of the season in not scoring for five games. Now, following Les Smith's corner, this was about to change. With his back to goal, big Roy received a difficult ball at waist height, controlled it with a fabulous touch before swivelling to hook the ball just inside the post, past the helpless Sanders. One of the great goals of all time.

# WEST BROMWICH ALBION v. WOLVES

Wolves might have got a second when Wilshaw's stunner hit Sanders on the chest. The ball bounced high into the air towards the goal, only to be caught by the Albion goalie as he fell backwards. For a moment, some of the crowd thought that Sanders may have carried the ball over the line. The referee obviously didn't think so, and play continued.

A stunned Albion tried hard to get back on terms through Joe Kennedy and Jimmy Dudley, with Paddy Ryan sending in a couple of long-range efforts. Freddie Cox at times showed his pace against Roy Pritchard, but it wasn't enough, and despite the brave show put up by Albion's reserves, Wolves had won both Black Country derbies that season.

Now the teams, both having played 37 games, were on level points, with 50 apiece. Albion stayed on top of the League, courtesy of their superior goal average, and were therefore still favourites for the title in the eyes of most soccer pundits. For their part, Wolves were now top scorers in the League.

The top of the table now looked like this:

|        | PLD | W  | D | L | F  | A  | PTS |
|--------|-----|----|---|---|----|----|-----|
| Albion | 37  | 21 | 8 | 8 | 83 | 51 | 50  |
| **Wolves** | 37 | 22 | 6 | 9 | 84 | 54 | 50 |

The ultimate destination of the League title now all depended on the final 5 games.

Meanwhile, on the same day at Hampden Park, in their first international since the Hungary humiliation and what was their final game in the Home International Championship/World Cup qualifier, England beat Scotland 4-2. The game was watched by a staggering 134,544 fans. England's goals came from Ivor Broadis, Johnny Nicholls, Ronnie Allen and Jimmy Mullen.

So once again, England had won the Home International Championship, and in the process had qualified for the World Cup finals in Switzerland. Despite being beaten, Scotland finished second and also qualified.

England: Merrick; Staniforth, Byrne; Wright (Capt.), Clarke, Dickinson; Finney, Broadis, Allen, Nicholls, Mullen.

On 6 April Wolves signed outside right Tommy McDonald from Hibernian. The speedy winger, who was in his early twenties, had already played for the Scottish B team.

A week later, the Baggies were off to South Wales to play Cardiff City, while Wolves took on Charlton at Molineux.

---

**West Bromwich Albion:** Sanders; Williams, Millard; Dudley, Dugdale, Kennedy; Cox, Ryan, Barlow, Carter, Cutler

**Wolves:** Williams; Stuart, Pritchard; Slater, Shorthouse, Flowers; Smith, Broadbent, Swinbourne, Wilshaw, Hancocks

# WOLVES V. CHARLTON ATHLETIC

**Football League Division One at Molineux**

**Date:** Saturday 10 April 1954         **Attendance:** 35,028

---

Billy Wright and Jimmy Mullen returned from their triumphant trip to Scotland with England, and seamlessly slotted back into the team, Billy once again at left-back. Every player knew that a good performance was needed against the Addicks if they were going to knock Albion off their lofty perch at the top of the League, and boy did they turn on the style.

They quickly brushed aside a couple of early Charlton attacks and cruised into top gear with a Johnny Hancocks 7th-minute thunderbolt that I'm sure Vince Bartram was pleased not to have got in the way of. Billy Wright started the move. Taking a short break from keeping Hurst quiet he calmly brought the ball out of defence and passed to Wilshaw, who chipped over a lovely ball for Swinbourne to nod down to Hancocks. The net bulged, 1-0! A minute later Hancocks sent over a peach of a cross for Dennis Wilshaw to head home.

Somehow, Charlton managed to hold out until the break, but in the second half came back under the screw, as Wolves tightened their hold on the game. Hancocks was having a brilliant game and might have – in fact should have – increased Charlton's agony, but instead of shooting on sight, he tried to shift the ball into an even better position and was crowded out.

In the 53rd minute, Wolves' two wonder-wingers combined to show how to pass accurately from wing to wing, resulting in another pin-point Hancocks pass back to Mullen, who beat Campbell before calmly rolling the ball into the Charlton goal. A minute before the hour, these terrible twins struck again, the ball whizzing from wing to wing in time-honoured fashion and then to Broadbent, who threaded the ball to the little right-winger. Disappointingly, this time Hancocks' centre failed to find a Wanderers head. Never mind, the ball skittered out to Mullen, who seemed to literally swivel in mid-air to meet it on the half-volley for his second of the game but strangely only his sixth of the season.

Wolves were now totally dominating the proceedings, with the visitors looking decidedly devastated, and in the 70th minute, they delivered the coup de grâce. This time it was Broadbent who, after some neat interplay, strode Hancocks-esque down the right flank to deliver an inch-perfect ball to Wolves' number seven. Hancocks met it perfectly to lash the ball home with his left foot. Just 2 minutes later, Eddie Firmani was adjudged to have handled the ball. Penalty, ruled the referee.

Hancocks eagerly grabbed the ball, intent on getting his second hat-trick of the season, but it was not to be, Johnny could never hold back on the power of his shooting, and on this occasion blazed the ball well wide. He reckoned that this was his first penalty miss since the one against Huddersfield three seasons earlier.

---

**Wolves 5**                                    **Charlton Athletic 0**

*Hancocks 2 (7 and 70),*
*Mullen 2 (53 and 59)*
*Wilshaw (8)*

# WOLVES *v*. CHARLTON ATHLETIC

Billy Wright in match action at Molineux.

Not long after this, Hancocks thumped a howitzer of a left-foot shot well over with only Bartram to beat. Charlton were well and truly beaten. On another day the score could have ended up resembling a cricket score, but we shouldn't grumble. Wolves were worthy winners. Finishing 5-0 was good enough for the new League leaders as well as boosting their goal-average tremendously.

On the radio, *Sports Report* was even more of a pleasure to listen to that evening because, surprisingly, Albion had lost 2-0 in Cardiff, and the mighty Wolves had gone top by 2 points. Wolves 52, Albion 50. Magic!

|        | PLD | W  | D | L | F  | A  | PTS |
|--------|-----|----|---|---|----|----|-----|
| **Wolves** | 38 | 23 | 6 | 9 | 89 | 54 | 52 |
| Albion | 38 | 21 | 8 | 9 | 83 | 53 | 50 |

---

**Wolves:** Williams; Stuart, Wright; Slater, Shorthouse, Flowers; Hancocks, Broadbent, Swinbourne, Wilshaw, Mullen

**Charlton Athletic:** Bartram; Campbell, Firmani; Hewie, Chamberlain, Hammond; Hurst, Ayre, Terry, White, Kiernan

# SHEFFIELD WEDNESDAY V. WOLVES

**Football League Division One at Hillsborough**

**Date:** Saturday 17 April 1954          **Attendance:** 41,278

---

A rare blank sheet. On only five previous occasions had Wolves failed to score in a match that season, although four of these had come since the turn of the year. It wasn't a dull game by any means, but it was a game in which, as most people predicted, Wolves could and should have disposed of the struggling Owls.

Despite being superior to Wednesday in every department, each of Wanderers' five forwards was guilty of frittering away good chances to score. It was an acutely depressing case of 'missing-the-target syndrome', for Broadbent in particular, who by the way, was otherwise once again quite magnificent. Peter sprayed the ball around accurately and intelligently to provide scoring opportunities that either his teammates contrived to miss or else were athletically saved by the excellent McIntosh in Wednesday's goal. The Owls' 'keeper never made a mistake, his most notable saves being a couple of great stops from Wilshaw and Swinbourne, plus others from Hancocks, Slater and Broadbent himself.

At the mid-point of the half, Hancocks raced clear, but with only McIntosh to beat he belted the ball for all he was worth, forsaking accuracy for power and allowing the Wednesday 'keeper to add to his already impressive string of top-class saves. Wolves' class was there for all to see, illuminating the gulf in skill between the two sets of players. Mind you, late in the half, a rare Owls foray up-field saw Froggatt sky one over the bar when he really should have hit the target; a big let-off for the visitors.

As the game wore on, Wolves regained the initiative, now looking a sure bet to wrap up both points. However, it was the home side that almost did it when Marriott's powerful shot was deflected towards Wolves' goal. Fortunately, the ball flew harmlessly over the bar. Up to now, each of Wolves' many efforts had ended with powerful shots that McIntosh had proved equal to. All too frequently, they demonstrated that they had singularly failed to learn the lessons of the first half.

First up, Peter Broadbent who, like Hancocks, opted for power; McIntosh dived full-length to push away his shot. The ball rolled into the path of Hancocks. Surely with the Owls' 'keeper still on the ground he couldn't miss this time? But rather than clip it over the prone 'keeper or slide it past him, once again he belted six kinds of something out of it. The ball flew towards the goal, hit McIntosh on the head and rebounded to safety.

Wanderers really should have won. They certainly threw away a futher point that was theirs for the taking. Billy Wright was once again flawless at left-back, but then again, he was always pretty good wherever and whenever he played. The same can be said for Bill Slater, who had a great game. Young Ron Flowers did well, showing more of the skill and power that promised so much

---

Sheffield Wednesday 0                    Wolves 0

# SHEFFIELD WEDNESDAY v. WOLVES

Eddie Stuart, Wolves.

for Wolves' future. We had definitely seen Swinbourne and Wilshaw play better, and the same goes for Hancocks and Mullen. Although to be fair, Owls' full-backs Kenny and Curtis certainly took no prisoners, often resorting to desperate methods to check the progress of Wanderers' wonder-wingers.

For Wednesday, the pick of the bunch were Gannon and O'Donnell, plus the mercurial Albert Quixall. Hopefully, Stan Cullis would introduce a degree of calmness into his side's next shooting practice session.

Wolves' solitary point at Hillsborough meant that they still led the division, despite Albion's 1-0 win at home to Manchester City, the goal coming from a Ronnie Allen penalty. It was still too close to call. Wolves 53 points, Albion 52.

|        | PLD | W  | D | L | F  | A  | PTS |
|--------|-----|----|---|---|----|----|-----|
| Wolves | 39  | 23 | 7 | 9 | 89 | 54 | 53  |
| Albion | 39  | 22 | 8 | 9 | 84 | 53 | 52  |

Now for the infamous Easter programme, where many a Championship has been won or lost. Albion's two games would be against mid-table local rivals Aston Villa. Wolves, however, had the daunting prospect of playing the team in third place.

---

**Sheffield Wednesday:** McIntosh; Kenny, Curtis; Gannon, O'Donnell, Davies; Marriot, Quixall, Shaw, Froggatt, Woodhead

**Wolves:** Williams; Stuart, Wright; Slater, Shorthouse, Flowers; Hancocks, Broadbent, Swinbourne, Wilshaw, Mullen

# Wolves v. Huddersfield Town

Football League Division One at Molineux

Date: Monday 19 April 1954                    Attendance: 42,862

A name familiar to all present-day Wolves' fans appeared on the Town team sheet – England wing-half Bill McGarry, later to manage Wolves on two separate occasions. McGarry epitomised the no-nonsense Huddersfield style of tough tackling, so this wasn't going to be easy. Former Wolves' full-back, local lad Larry Kelly was given the honour of captaining the visitors against his former club.

The third-highest gate of the season piled into Molineux in good spirits, anticipating a thrilling game between the League leaders and the team in third place. They certainly weren't disappointed. The game kicked off at 3 p.m. on a bright, sunny, warm day, with Wolves swarming onto the attack from the off. They were all over Town like a rash.

On 2 minutes another Johnny Hancocks cannonball cross-cum-shot was deflected into the path of Jimmy Mullen, who powered a low shot into the net to open the scoring for Wolves. Town's first real attack forced Billy Wright to be alert to clear the ball off the line with Williams beaten.

Both teams swung the ball from wing to wing providing the good-sized crowd with a great deal of pleasure, even more so when, in the 27th minute, Wolves were awarded a penalty for a foul on Dennis Wilshaw. Hancocks ran up, and blow me down; he missed again from 12 yards. On this occasion, his thunderball of a shot whistled wide of a post. This was unheard of – two recent penalties, two misses.

On 35 minutes, Hancocks atoned for his penalty miss with a wicked narrow-angle free-kick from fully 35 yards out that fizzed past Jack Wheeler, the ball bulging the Town net to almost breaking point to send the home side in 2-0 up at the interval.

Soon after the restart, Bill Slater got a bang on the head, but was okay after Joe Gardiner's magic sponge had taken effect. Then Jimmy Mullen watched in horror as his seemingly goalbound shot rolled along the goal line before spinning out. A couple of minutes later Ron Flowers screwed a rocket shot wide from 25 yards out. More misses from Wolves followed, but really it was all one-way traffic.

England full-back Staniforth and his partner Kelly were excellent for Town and made sure that their colleagues never gave up the fight. In the 85th minute, the Huddersfield goalkeeper had to leave the field following a collision. Centre forward Jim Glazzard took over between the sticks, effectively ending Town's chances of getting anything from this game, and although he did okay, making a few brave saves, in the dying minutes Wolves grabbed two more.

First, it was the stylish architect of most Wolves' attacks, Peter Broadbent. Peter scored with a fine 88th-minute header from Mullen's corner after the bounce of the ball had deceived Glazzard. Then, a minute later, Dennis Wilshaw crashed a too-hot-to-hold loose ball into the roof of Town's net to

---

**Wolves 4**                              **Huddersfield Town 0**

Mullen (2), Broadbent (88)
Hancocks (35)
Wilshaw (89)

Huddersfield's Bill McGarry heads the ball clear.

give a great boost to Wolves' goal average. But this was not before Burrell had flashed in a dangerous cross that was only stopped with perfect timing by Billy Wright.

The final 4-0 scoreline may well have flattered Wolves a little, but as they say where I come from, 'It's them uz guzz in uz counts!' Billy Wright was once again commanding in Wolves' defence.

With these 2 points, and Albion only managing a 1-1 home draw with Villa, courtesy of a goal from Nicholls, Wolves opened up a nice 2-point gap at the top. With only 2 games and 4 points left to play for, things were looking decidedly good for the western half of the Black Country. Next day's results were crucial.

| | PLD | W | D | L | F | A | PTS |
|---|---|---|---|---|---|---|---|
| **Wolves** | 40 | 24 | 7 | 9 | 93 | 54 | 55 |
| Albion | 40 | 22 | 9 | 9 | 85 | 54 | 53 |

**Wolves:** Williams; Stuart, Wright; Slater, Shorthouse, Flowers; Hancocks, Broadbent, Swinbourne, Wilshaw, Mullen

**Huddersfield Town:** Wheeler; Staniforth, Kelly; McGarry, McEvoy, Battye; Burrell, Cavanagh, Glazzard, Watson, Frear

# Huddersfield Town v. Wolves

**Football League Division One at Leeds Road**

**Date:** Tuesday 20 April 1954          **Attendance:** 35,841 (10,000 Wolves' fans)

Some Wolves fans maybe thought it was already all over, but it's a funny old game this football! Fate often has a nasty habit of biting the over-optimistic among us in the most horrible places. Wolves certainly got bitten on this dull day in Huddersfield!

Thousands of the faithful took the trouble to make the long and tiring journey up north – remember there were no motorways in those days – in the knowledge that their 'Golden Boys' needed only 1 point to secure the League Championship for the first time ever. Today would not be a day for the faint-hearted. Everyone in Wolverhampton and the surrounding towns had everything crossed, hoping and praying that their team would hold their nerve. Wolves were unchanged for the fourth game in a row and won the toss.

Understandably, with so much at stake it was a nervy-looking Wolves that began the game. When they went a goal down after 4 minutes, this did nothing to ease the tension. Wolves regrouped and attacked in force, forcing a corner following a mini blitzkrieg on the Town goal. Many of Wolves' players were still in and around the Huddersfield penalty area when the ball reached Town's left-half Battye, who belted it up field as far as he could. Bill Shorthouse misjudged the ball as he ran to meet it, allowing it to bounce over him into the path of Jim Glazzard, who was able to run on and place a fine shot wide of Williams. Actually, it was more of a tap than a shot. This was Huddersfield's first attack.

Wolves recovered a little of their composure and came back at Town with a vengeance. Wilshaw got the ball into the Town net only for the goal to be disallowed for offside. The linesman raised his flag high into the air. Seeing this, full-back Ron Staniforth grabbed the ball in both hands a split second before the referee blew his whistle. Technically this should have been a penalty, but the ref waved away Wolves' protests.

On 16 minutes, Mullen waltzed down the left wing and whizzed in a cracking cross to Hancocks, who spotted Mills off his line. Taking careful aim, Johnny tried to hit the top corner, but Kelly had anticipated his intention and managed to get his foot in the way of the shot to block the ball out for a corner. Just before this, Broadbent had thumped a fierce cross-shot against Mills' legs and the ball had bounced away from danger.

Huddersfield appeared to be content to let Wolves come at them, using the offside trap as an effective weapon, and thwarting many a Wolves raid. Offside traps are there to be sprung, and in the 27th minute Roy Swinbourne did just that. Timing his late run to perfection, he strode through on goal, but with plenty of time to steady himself chose to shoot before he was set and blazed the ball high and wide. He repeated this 3 minutes later, racing past McEvoy with consummate ease to

---

**Huddersfield Town 2**
*Glazzard (4)*
*McGarry (63)*

**Wolves 1**
*Wilshaw (43)*

place an excellent shot past Mills, or so the fans thought. Unfortunately, the Town goalie managed to stick out a foot to divert the ball away from goal to, in the end, trickle agonisingly the wrong side of the post as far as Wolves were concerned.

Swinbourne was certainly on fire, and he burst through again, only to be foiled once more when his shot was charged down. Wolves were now controlling this game, but were having no luck in front of goal. Swinbourne broke clear again in the 37th minute to send in a stinger of a shot that Mills could only parry. The ball fizzed around the box for a while, all attempts at a clearance failing. Eventually the ball came to Wilshaw, who crashed in a ferocious drive that Kelly managed to head against an upright and the ball spun clear.

Desperate Huddersfield just about managed to hold out until the closing minutes of the half. But then Wolves got back into the game with a 43rd-minute tap-in goal by Dennis Wilshaw, following a powerful thrusting run by Bill Slater that had resulted in a goalmouth mêlée.

Wolves started the second period looking as though they now believed they could win this game, and went close with fine efforts from Swinbourne, Wilshaw and Hancocks, any of which might have produced a goal. Just after the hour mark, Wolves' future manager Bill McGarry snuffed out Wanderers' candle with a tremendous long-range crackerjack of a free-kick to restore Town's lead. To add insult to injury, many thought that the ball was moving when he leathered it.

'Fight, fight, wherever you may be' became Wolves' watchword as they strove to get back on terms, but sadly it was not to be. For the remainder of the match Huddersfield defended stoutly and looked dangerous on the break; Wolves couldn't conjure up a goal no matter how hard they tried. In effect, the game was all over bar the shouting.

Albion's League campaign was pretty much ended by rampant near-neighbours Aston Villa. The Villains dished out a right royal 6-1 thrashing of their near neighbours at Villa Park, five goals coming in the first 35 minutes. Albion's consolation goal was scored by Griffin. So now it was pretty much all over as far as the Championship was concerned. With only one match remaining, Wolves proudly sat at the top of the League with 55 points compared to Albion's 53.

The goal average pendulum had also swung in Wolves' favour with a goals total of 94 for and 56 against, with the Baggies goals at 86 for and 60 against – amazing what difference a few games can make.

| | PLD | W | D | L | F | A | PTS |
|---|---|---|---|---|---|---|---|
| **Wolves** | **41** | **24** | **7** | **10** | **94** | **56** | **55** |
| Albion | 41 | 22 | 9 | 10 | 86 | 60 | 53 |

The race for third and fourth place was still on. Huddersfield Town were due to play Bolton Wanderers at Leeds Road on the following Saturday in the game that would settle this. With Manchester United snapping at their heels, a number of the final games of the season had even more of an edge to them.

On the eve of Wolves' final game, the youth team travelled to Old Trafford, Manchester, to play the first leg of the 1953/54 FA Youth Cup final.

This competition had been inaugurated the season before, when Wolves had been beaten in the final by Manchester United by a staggering 9 goals to 3 aggregate. Now, on the evening of Friday

# HUDDERSFIELD TOWN v. WOLVES

Duncan Edwards, Manchester United

23 April 1954, in front of a crowd of 18,246, the two best youth teams in the country locked horns in the second final of this prestigious competition.

After only 5 minutes, United took an early lead through a Duncan Edwards header. It was then that Wolves' cubs really got down to business. Goals from Joe Bonson, Jimmy Murray and Bobby Mason put Wolves 3-1 up in what was a scintillating first-half display. In the second half, United doggedly stuck to their task, and were eventually rewarded when the referee awarded them a disputed penalty.

Edwards had gone down in the box from no more than the slightest of contact with centre half Timmins. We subsequently learned that the penalty had been for handball. The goal spurred United on to double their efforts. Edwards powered in a headed goal that was almost a repeat of his earlier effort, and suddenly the score was back to 3-3. Wolves charged forward and wing half Fallon put Wanderers back in front. Unfortunately, the Reds wouldn't lie down and Dave Pegg got his second of the game to bring the scores, and the result, level at 4-4. The second leg would be played at Molineux on the following Monday.

Now for the final game of the season, and what a day it promised to be at Molineux! With the League title already effectively sewn up, Wolves could relax and put on a show for all their loyal fans.

By contrast, and almost certainly, it was a dejected Albion that travelled to the South Coast to play Pompey in their final game of the season, knowing that only a combination of two miracles could prevent Wolves from being crowned Champions of England. To have any chance at all of winning the title, the Baggies not only needed to win at Portsmouth and in the process run up a cricket score, but Wolves would have to lose by a hatful. Surely an impossible scenario? There was much speculation surrounding the various combinations of results that Albion would have to get in order to pip Wolves. One of the daftest was: if Wolves lost 1-0, Albion would win the title if they could beat Portsmouth 13-0! Crackers or what?

---

**Huddersfield Town:** Mills; Staniforth, Kelly; McGarry, McEvoy, Battye; Burrell, Cavanagh, Glazzard, Davie, Frear

**Wolves:** Williams; Stuart, Wright; Slater, Shorthouse, Flowers; Hancocks, Broadbent, Swinbourne, Wilshaw, Mullen

# Wolves v. Tottenham Hotspur

**Football League Division One at Molineux**

**Date:** Saturday 24 April 1954                    **Attendance:** 44,055

Unchanged again for the fifth time in five games, Wolves just needed to have the official endorsement stamped on their Champions-elect name tag, and there was no way that anyone was going to spoil this party. Wolves and Wolverhampton were going to enjoy this monumental and historic day.

Another large crowd turned up for the celebrations, pretty much everyone relaxed and happy, unlike the nervy nonsense at Sheffield and Huddersfield. Actually, the game turned out to be a bit of an anticlimax. What we got was a rather sedate and friendly, gentlemanly kind of game, rather than the football skill-fest that we hoped would accompany our first ever Championship. Despite the abundance of 'niceness', it didn't take the 'Golden Aces' long to add to the anticipated spectacle.

On 18 minutes, Bill Slater sent Hancocks racing away down the right. Another fantastic cross-field ball to the opposite wing followed, which Jimmy Mullen controlled in an instant, before sending over a cross of slide-rule precision that easily beat the leaden-footed Harry Clarke, and there was Roy Swinbourne rising majestically above the Spurs centre half to power a scintillating header past Ted Ditchburn. A classic Wolves goal.

The big Spurs' 'keeper was then called upon to make a series of fine saves from Swinbourne and Wilshaw, before a defender's legs on Spurs' goal line stopped a tornado of a shot from Slater. Just after this, Dunmore forced a corner for Spurs and it looked for a moment like the visitors had equalised. Fortunately for Wanderers, Walters was judged to be offside when he was first to a neat through-ball before flicking the ball past Bert Williams. The linesman was flagging long before Walters put it in. Even the match officials were doing the right thing for a change; they were obviously in a generous mood.

1-0 at the interval was a fair scoreline on the basis of play. In the second period, it was confirmed to Tottenham that this was to be Wolves' day. McClellan burst through the centre of Wolves' defence, looking odds-on to score. Bert Williams was having none of it, and advanced from his goal to block the danger, parrying the Spurs man's shot before grabbing the ball at the second attempt. Then it was Roy Swinbourne again for Wolves to make it 2-0.

Some great interplay saw Mullen and Wilshaw exchange passes ending with the left-winger arrowing his centre to Swinbourne's head with incredible precision. One wondered if he could actually send the ball over with the lace on the opposite side to that which Big Roy would meet with his head; fanciful stuff indeed. Roy's header had the distinction of being Wolves' final goal of the campaign.

---

**Wolves 2**                    **Tottenham Hotspur 0**

*Swinbourne 2 (18 and 68)*

'Wolves, clear-cut Champions!' *Sporting Star* headline.

In a 73rd-minute scramble, Eddie Stuart almost made it three, but unfortunately, he screwed the ball wide, and anyway, it didn't really matter. Ted Ditchburn in Spurs' goal produced an acrobatic display to entertain the crowd. His best save came from another great Swinbourne header that he tipped over the crossbar, but in the end even he couldn't prevent the Champions elect from grabbing their first ever League title.

The referee's final whistle was the signal for tens of thousands of Wolves' fans to invade the pitch. They wanted to congratulate the players and get the best vantage point that they could for the trophy presentation that some believed was to follow; Molineux had never seen anything like it.

Fifty or so Wolverhampton coppers knew that they were powerless to prevent the onrushing hoards, so they sensibly stepped out of the way, opting instead to make a passageway for the players and officials to leave the field, which the lads did, to a gauntlet of well-deserved backslapping. There was no malice in the fans, only pure unadulterated joy. Eventually, the players and officials managed to struggle off the pitch and to the dressing room without mishap; however the fans certainly hadn't had enough. They wanted to see their heroes, needed to unleash the proud adulation beating in their breasts. The chant 'we want Wolves, we want Wolves' echoed around Molineux, but still the players failed to reappear.

The fans pressed forward still chanting. It was as though no one had thought through this moment, and decided beforehand what should be done. In the end, it was Wolves' announcer Ted Kenny who rescued the embarrassing situation. Over the loudspeaker he promised the fans a second view of their heroes, asking them to be patient, and thereby calming the excited masses.

A few minutes later, with the crowd still buzzing with excitement, Billy Wright led his gallant team, some now dressed in tracksuits, up the short flight of steps to the director's box, before taking the microphone to say a few words to emphasise what this meant to the club, to the players and staff and to Billy himself. He summed it all up in a sentence, 'It's been a struggle. We shall try to do our best for you next season.'

The ecstatic crowd called for Stan Cullis, but he didn't appear, remaining firmly in the background, dignified and proud; no doubt wanting his players to take all the credit and glory. The loudspeaker announced that the First Division Championship Trophy would be officially presented to Wolves by the President of the Football League after the playing of the second leg of the FA Youth Cup final between Wolves and Manchester United at Molineux on Monday evening.

So that was it, we'd won the First Division Championship.

Sadly for the Albion, they lost 3-0 at Portsmouth to miss out on the chance of becoming the first club in modern times to win the coveted double – League Championship and FA Cup in the same season. There seems little doubt that during the run-in, the Baggies players all had one eye on the Cup final, each wanting to avoid injury – and who can blame them? They had literally thrown away the League title that with 7 games to go they were odds-on to win. Maybe the loss of their crippled goalkeeper Norman Heath affected them; certainly losing their key strikers for both the Sunderland and Wolves games must have been a bitter pill to swallow for manager Vic Buckingham and his fine side.

But we shouldn't dwell on any negative aspects, because 1953/54 turned out to be fantastically successful for Black Country football, Wolves winning the First Division Championship for the first time in their history, and West Bromwich Albion winning the FA Cup. A full house for the Black Country.

Two days after the Tottenham game, on the evening of Monday 26 April 1954, Molineux was the setting for the return leg of the FA Youth Cup final between Wolves and Manchester United. Unfortunately, once again Wolves' lads weren't able to overcome this set of even younger Busby Babes, missing out narrowly 1-0 to a Dave Pegg penalty in a tense game. The 1-0 scoreline on the night meant that Wolves' lads had lost by the aggregate score of 5-4. A crowd of 28,651 had turned out to watch this match, and of course to witness the presentation of the Trophies that followed the game. The FA Youth Cup Trophy was presented to United by Joe Richards, Chairman of the FA Youth Cup Committee.

Then the partisan crowd went wild as up stepped League President Arthur Drewry to present the First Division Championship Trophy to Billy Wright who told the fans 'It's going to take a darned good team to take this trophy from us.' The crowd once again shouted for Stan Cullis, and this time the great man appeared. He thanked the fans for their support, so loyally given during a difficult and successful season. The final trophy to be presented was the Birmingham League Shield, whose President J.T. Stone handed it to third-team coach, Billy Crook. Then it was all over; Wolves had been officially crowned Champions of England for the first time in their history. A monumental occasion and a monumental achievement.

The local press announced that a celebration banquet at the civic hall had been arranged for 10 May. Tickets were priced at £2 10s for those who wished to attend and who could afford it.

# Wolves v. Tottenham Hotspur

A few days later, Wolves left for a three-match tour of Denmark and Sweden, where they would play against teams from Aarhus, Helsingborg and Copenhagen. Missing from the trip would be Billy Wright and Jimmy Mullen, who were due to play for the Football League against the Scottish League at Stamford Bridge on Wednesday 28 April 1954. Also staying behind were Bill Slater and Dennis Wilshaw. Both players were to join the FA Party after the game for the trip to Yugoslavia and Hungary, ahead of the World Cup finals in June. Bert Williams and Johnny Hancocks were also unable to make the Scandinavian trip. So it was a weakened Wolves that beat Aarhus and Helsingborg HAF by the same 5-0 scoreline, and earned a 2-2 draw in the Danish capital.

Bill Slater didn't make it into the England squad for the World Cup finals; his first full cap would eventually come in November 1954. However, Wolves were well represented in Switzerland by Wright, Mullen and Wilshaw. England lost 4-2 to Uruguay in the quarter-final.

At Wembley on 1 May 1954, West Bromwich Albion beat Preston North End 3-2, with two goals from Ronnie Allen (one penalty), plus one from Frank Griffin. Over the season Allen had scored 27 League goals, plus 7 in the Cup to total 34 goals in all competitions. Nicholls got 28 League, plus 4 Cup goals to finish with 32, a staggering 66 goals between them.

Coming up later for Wolves' fans in 1954 were the floodlight matches at Molineux that sealed Wanderers' world-wide reputation as one the planet's top teams: a disappointing 0-0 draw with First Vienna of Austria on 13 October, the 10-0 thrashing of Maccabi Tel-Aviv on 28 October and the 4-0 drubbing of Spartak Moscow on 16 November. And then the big one, when the amazing Magyar soccer machine came to town, the team of the Hungarian Army, Honved of Budapest.

Wolves' fantastic fighting 3-2 victory over Honved on 13 December 1954, with two goals from Roy Swinbourne and one from Johnny Hancocks, saw them unofficially crowned Kings of World Soccer; a fitting tribute to Stan Cullis and his marvellous Wolves players. The Honved team including six of the seven members of Hungary's fabulous international side that in 1952 were crowned Olympic Champions, the same Mighty Magyar side that were unlucky to lose the 1954 World Cup final to West Germany by three goals to two. This was also the team that had emphatically beaten England 6-3 at Wembley to become the very first non-British Isles team to beat England on home soil, and that, in May 1954, had humiliated England 7-1 in Budapest.

**Wolves:** Williams; Stuart, Wright; Slater, Shorthouse, Flowers; Hancocks, Broadbent, Swinbourne, Wilshaw, Mullen

**Tottenham Hotspur:** Ditchburn; Baker, Willis; Nicholson, Clarke, Wetton; Walters, Bennett, Dunmore, Baily, McClellan

# 1953/54 Statistics

1953/54 final top two League placings:

|         | PLD | W  | D | L | F  | A  | W | D | L | F  | A  | PTS |
|---------|-----|----|---|---|----|----|---|---|---|----|----|-----|
| **Wolves** | 42  | 16 | 3 | 4 | 61 | 25 | 9 | 6 | 6 | 35 | 31 | 57  |
| Albion  | 42  | 13 | 5 | 3 | 51 | 24 | 9 | 4 | 8 | 35 | 39 | 53  |

Huddersfield Town finished in third place with 51 points, with Manchester United fourth and Bolton Wanderers fifth, both on 48 points. At the other end of the table, Liverpool on 28 points and Middlesbrough on 30 points were relegated to the Second Division.

Wolves used twenty-two players in this, their first Championship-winning season.

The players:

**Bert Williams**, *goalkeeper (34 League appearances in 1953/54).*

Bert Williams, Wolves' marvellous and ever-popular goalkeeper, affectionately nicknamed the 'Cat', finally hung up his gloves at the end of the 1956/57 season after making 420 senior appearances. He retired to concentrate on running his successful sports shop in Bilston, the town where he was born on 31 January 1920. A Walsall Town find, for whom he played 28 times, the acrobatic Bert joined Wolves for a fee of £3,500 in September 1945, making his debut on the 22nd of that month in a wartime Football League (South) game against Chelsea. During the Second World War he served with the RAF. Between 1949 and 1955 he played in goal for England in 24 internationals, including the 1950 World Cup finals, where he lined up with Billy Wright. Bert kept goal in all three of England's group matches, including the ill-fated and humiliating 1-0 defeat by the USA. Bert Williams also played in goal for England during the war, as well as winning an England B cap, and playing 5 times for the Football League. His Wolves career was littered with achievements, including an FA Cup winner's medal in 1949 and the First Division Championship in 1953/54, along with those glorious floodlight victories at Molineux.

**John (Jack) Short**, *right-back (26 League appearances in 1953/54).*

Born in Barnsley on 18 February 1928, John, sometimes known as Jack, joined Wolves at the age of seventeen from Wolves' nursery club Wath Wanderers, making his senior debut on 2 December 1950 at Molineux in the 3-1 win against West Bromwich Albion; his first of 107 first-team outings before transferring to Stoke City in August 1954. He later joined his home team Barnsley, before retiring in May 1960. Sadly, he died in 1976.

# 1953/54 Statistics

**Roy Pritchard**, *left-back (27 League appearances in 1953/54).*

Roy was born in Dawley, Shropshire on 9 May 1925, joining Wolves in August 1945. He made his professional debut on 12 October 1946 against Huddersfield Town. He transferred to Aston Villa in February 1946 after making 223 senior appearances in a Wolves shirt. He subsequently played for Notts County, Port Vale and non-League Wellington Town before retiring in 1964; he died in March 1993.

**Bill Slater**, *right half (39 League appearances, 2 goals in 1953/54).*

A footballer of real quality and a gentleman of great dignity, Bill Slater OBE CBE played 12 times for the full England team, and 21 times for England at amateur level, turning out 339 times for Wolves, in the process scoring 25 goals. Bill was born in the Lancashire town of Clitheroe on 29 April 1927, and joined Blackpool Town in 1944, for whom he scored 9 goals in 30 appearances. During this time he also turned out for Yorkshire Amateurs and Leeds University. As an amateur, Bill Slater had the distinction of playing at Wembley at inside left for Blackpool in the 1951 FA Cup final, where they were beaten 2-0 by Newcastle United. In December 1952 he moved to Brentford, from where he joined Wolves. The story goes that after getting a lecturing job with Birmingham University he travelled to Wolves to ask if he could play for them; of course, the answer was a resounding yes, and the rest, as they say, is history, as Slater became one of the club's most prized assets. In February 1954 Bill became a part-time professional and went on to play in Wolves' successive League Championship-winning teams in 1957/58 and 1958/59, captaining Wolves' FA Cup-winning side of 1959/60, voted footballer of the year and gaining his BSc also in that year. He left Wolves in the 1963 close season, rejoining Brentford for a season before moving to Northern Nomads, from where he retired towards the end in 1964. Subsequently, he became deputy director of the Crystal Palace sports centre, before taking on the role of director of physical education at Liverpool and Birmingham Universities. He was awarded the OBE in 1982 and the CBE in 1998 for his services to sport. In 1984 he was elected president of the British Gymnastics Association. Like teammate Billy Wright, Bill Slater was never cautioned in a long and distinguished career; surely a giant among sportsmen all over the world.

**Bill Shorthouse**, *centre half and left-back (40 League appearances in 1953/54).*

Another Wolves stalwart, centre half and left-back Bill Shorthouse decided to retire through injury in the summer of 1957. Bill had been Wolves' captain before Billy Wright took on the role, playing in 376 senior games, scoring 1 goal. Born in Bilston on 22 May 1922, he joined Wolves as an amateur in April 1945, having been a member of the British Expeditionary Force. He was wounded in the Normandy D-Day landing. Bill spend some time with Wath Wanderers, where he honed his skills to those needed to play at the topmost level, making his senior debut against Manchester City at Maine Road on 23 August 1947. In his long career at Wolves he had the distinction of never having been dropped. He retired after the 3-0 victory over Birmingham City on 29 September 1956, to concentrate on coaching. Bill went on to become coach of the England Youth team in the 1960s before coaching at Birmingham City, and in 1980 coached Aston Villa to their FA Youth Cup triumph.

**Billy Wright**, *left half, centre half, right-back and left-back (39 League appearances in 1953/54).*

Ironbridge-born Billy Wright CBE was a marvellous man, a true ambassador of the sport and a truly great footballer. For Wolves, he made a total of 541 appearances, scoring 16 goals. He joined the groundstaff in 1938, after initially being turned down by Major Buckley for being too small. He made his debut against West Bromwich Albion in the 5-3 defeat at The Hawthorns on 23 September 1939, before turning professional in 1941. Born in Ironbridge on 6 February 1924, Billy went on to win 105 full England caps, his first in 1946, captaining England on 90 occasions, and playing in the finals of 3 World Cups. He also won an England B cap and was selected for the Football League on 21 occasions. And of course, he won an FA Cup and three First Division Championships with Wolves. In his exemplary twenty-year first-class career Billy was never booked or sent off. A great man, a great Wolves captain. It was at the start of the 1959/60 season that this Wolves legend, then aged thirty-five, dropped a bombshell by announcing his retirement. He reputedly told a reporter, 'Yes, this is it. I have had a wonderful run with a wonderful club and I want to finish while I am still at the top.' Stan Cullis was reported to have said that under no circumstances would he ask Billy to play in the Central League team; he wanted him to finish as a first-team player. Billy played his farewell match at Molineux in Wolves colours in the pre-season charity practice match on Saturday 8 August 1959. Although Billy's news was bad for Wolves it was good for charity, as a larger than normal number of fans was expected to turn out in honour of their captain. In fact, 20,000, twice the usual, came to Molineux to witness Billy's swansong. The game was an emotional affair, with the players forming a guard of honour. As a mark of respect, Billy was switched from the Whites – the second eleven – to the Colours – the first team – for his last Molineux match. The Whites won 4-2. Bobby Mason and Jimmy Murray put the Colours 2-0 up, but before the interval Barry Stobart pulled one back for the Whites. After the break, Des Horne levelled with a penalty then scored the goal of the match, after Colin Booth had given the Whites the lead. The Whites' half-back line of Slater, Showell and Kirkham looked every bit as good as the Colours' England trio of Clamp, Wright and Flowers. In a later interview, Billy Wright acknowledged that he had told reporters the previous April that he reckoned he was good for another season at least, but added that, since he had got his England hundred and had been awarded the CBE, he had thought it over and decided now was the time to quit. He reminded people that Wolves' policy was based upon the development of younger players, and felt that the time had come to make way for George Showell to take his place in the team. He added that one thing he was certain about was that George would make a good job of it. Stan Cullis wanted Billy to take over as his chief coach, with specific responsibility for coaching the club's youngsters. Billy hadn't yet decided, but had confirmed that he would not move to another club. 'How can I play for anyone else after Wolves?' he said. Billy's third benefit cheque, this time for £1,000, was due in October. What more can be said about Billy Wright CBE that hasn't already been said? Another true gentleman, he always had time to sign autographs, always had time for the fans. Voted Footballer of the Year in 1951/52 and runner-up European Footballer of the Year in 1956/57, Billy won everything and achieved everything in his long and illustrious career. He was the David Beckham of his day, captain of England and married to one of the best-known faces in show-business, Joy Beverley of the Beverley Sisters singing trio. Elected a life member of the FA, Billy was the rock that Stan Cullis built his team around. In October 1960, he was appointed manager of the England Youth team and after this manager of England Under-23s. He went on to manage Arsenal in May 1962 before becoming Head of Sport at ATV, and then Central TV, and subsequently a director of his beloved Wolverhampton Wanderers. Sadly Billy Wright died, aged seventy, on 3 September 1994; a great loss to England and sport in general.

# 1953/54 STATISTICS

**Johnny Hancocks**, *outside right and outside left (42 League appearances, 24 goals in 1953/54).*
Born in Oakengates on 30 April 1919, Johnny was the only player ever-present in Wolves' first Championship-winning season, all but one game at outside right. In the close season of 1957, Johnny Hancocks retired from the full-time professional game; he was thirty-eight years old. Sad for me, because he was one of my all-time favourite players. In 1956/57 Harry Hooper had taken over Johnny's right-wing berth in the first eleven, but the little man wasn't through yet. I remember watching him play for the reserves, still the darling of the fans, scoring 24 goals in the Central League that season. At 5ft 4ins, Johnny Hancocks was one of the smallest players around; however, he packed an explosive shot into his size-four boots. Johnny's record was incredible for a winger. In all competitions, he scored 168 goals in 378 senior games for Wolves. He joined Walsall Town from Oakengates Town just before the start of the Second World War, serving as an Army PT instructor during the hostilities. He signed for Wolves on 11 May 1946 for a fee of £4,000, making his debut against Arsenal in a 6-1 win at Molineux on 31 August 1946, scoring 10 League goals and 1 in the Cup in his first season. This great player won 3 full England caps, scoring twice on his international debut, and also played for the Football League. He played his last first-team game for Wolves on 3 April 1956 against Aston Villa at Villa Park in a 0-0 draw, but briefly returned to the fray on the night of Tuesday 11 December 1956 for the last 8 minutes of the 1-1-drawn floodlit friendly against MTK of Budapest, otherwise known as Red Banner. He finally hung up his boots at the ripe old footballing age of 38, when he moved to Wellington Town, now Telford United, as player/manager in the 1957 close season. Johnny Hancocks was top-scorer for Wolves on 3 separate occasions, jointly with Jesse Pye in 1947/48 with 16 goals, 1954/55 with 27, and 1955/57 with 18. His 24 League goals in the 1953/54 Championship-winning season put him in joint second place in the Wolves goal-scoring charts with Roy Swinbourne. Johnny subsequently managed Southern League club Cambridge United before returning to his home town to work for local company GKN Sankey. Johnny Hancocks died on 19 February 1994, two months short of his seventy-fifth birthday.

**Peter Broadbent**, *inside right and inside left (36 League appearances, 12 goals in 1953/54).*
The silky skills of inside forward Peter Broadbent graced the Molineux stage for 14 years. Stan Cullis signed him from Brentford for £10,000 in February 1951 after only playing 16 games for the Bees, calling it one of his finest ever signings. He was a magical playmaker, a great passer of the ball and a brilliant goal-scorer. His delicate touch and outstanding body-swerve rivalled anything seen in Continental football. Peter Broadbent's style of play attracted numerous admirers, including the illustrious George Best. In Joe Lovejoy's book *Bestie*, Wolves fan George says that he didn't have an individual hero, but supposed that Broadbent was close. Yes – as a boy George Best supported Wolves. Born in Elvington, Kent on 15 May 1933. Broadbent subsequently came to the attention of the football world while playing for Dover, from where he moved to Brentford in 1950. Peter Broadbent won 3 First Division Championships and 1 FA Cup with Wolves, plus 7 full international caps with England, his first in the 1958 World Cup finals in Sweden. He also represented England at Under-23 and B level, and played for Young England and the Football League. In total, Peter made 497 senior appearances for Wolves, scoring 145 goals. Sadly, Peter Broadbent left the club in January 1965 when he joined Shrewsbury Town, before subsequently moving to Aston Villa, Stockport County and Bromsgrove Rovers, retiring in 1971.

**Roy Swinbourne**, *centre forward (40 League appearances, 24 goals in 1953/54).*

Hailing from Denbigh Main in Yorkshire, where he was born on 25 August 1929, Roy Swinbourne had been hailed the new king of Molineux following his haul of 20-plus goals in seasons 1950/51 and 1952/53. His 24 goals for the 1953/54 Championship-winning team and his two against Honved cemented his place in Wolves' goalscoring history. The son of a former Aston Villa reserve full-back, Roy was a product of Wolves nursery club Wath Wanderers, where he was sent by Wolves as a fifteen-year-old, making his first-team debut for Wolves in the 1-1 home draw with Fulham on 17 December 1949, scoring his first goal for Wolves nine days later in the 3-2 defeat at Molineux by Aston Villa on Boxing Day. He was Wolves' top scorer in 1950/51, with 22 goals from 48 League and Cup games, but missed half of the following season, scoring only 4 in 20 appearances. In 1952/53 he was again top scorer with 21 goals from 42 games. Disappointingly, in the season following Wolves' first Championship, 1954/55, Roy only managed 18 in 41 starts. His popularity was further cemented in the 1955/56 season, when he scored 17 in the first 12 games. His exploits included scoring 4 in the 7-2 home destruction of Manchester City in August, plus hat-tricks in the record 9-1 away win against Cardiff City in September, and in the 4-0 annihilation of Huddersfield at Molineux. On 5 November 1955, in a cruel twist of fate, Swinbourne was injured in a match at Luton Town while trying to hurdle a group of official photographers at the side of the goal, a game which unhappily Wolves lost 5-1. Unfortunately, in his comeback match at Preston on 3 December, after missing 3 games, he broke down and was never able to play again. There seems little doubt that an injury-free Roy Swinbourne would have gone on to be an even greater all-time legend, and at twenty-six years of age surely it would have been only a matter of time before he won his first international cap with England. His only international honour was an England B cap against West Germany in 1954/55. There is no doubt that Wolves sorely missed his goal flair at the end of the 1954/55 season when they finished in second place behind Champions Chelsea, Roy missing the final 6 games through injury. With him in the team Wolves might have won back-to-back League titles. The same might be said for the following season, when Wolves finished in third place on goal average. We'll never know. In all, Roy scored 114 goals in 230 games for Wolves, including seven hat-tricks and those 2 memorable goals in the victory over the mighty Honved.

**Dennis Wilshaw**, *inside left (39 League appearances, the club's top scorer with 26 League goals in 1953/54, plus 1 in the FA Cup).*

Schoolmaster Dennis Wilshaw was born in Stoke-on-Trent on 11 March 1926 and signed professional forms for Wolves in 1944. After a successful loan spell with Walsall in 1946/47, he was recalled to Molineux in 1948, scoring 10 that season in 11 outings, including a hat-trick on his first-team debut in the 3-0 defeat of Newcastle United on 12 March 1949. In all for Wolves he scored 112 goals in 219 games, plus 5 in 13 matches during the war. He was transferred to Stoke City in December 1957, where he went on to score 49 goals for the Potters until 1961, when at the age of thirty-five a broken leg forced him to retire from the game. He played in 12 full England internationals, including the 1954 World Cup finals in Switzerland, scoring 10 goals; he also won 2 England B caps. In April 1955, in his fourth game for his country, Dennis Wilshaw scored a record-breaking 4 goals for England in the 7-2 demolition of Scotland at Wembley, playing in an England team that also included Billy Wright and Bert Williams. In the summer of 1955, Wolves played and lost 2 friendlies in Moscow, Spartak getting their revenge for the Molineux defeat by beating Wolves 3-0 on 7 August. Then, Wolves went down 3-2 to Moscow Dynamo five days later. In that match, Dennis Wilshaw scored both Wolves goals, becoming the first Englishman to score in Russia. Another record to add to his four goals against Scotland. Dennis Wilshaw sadly died earlier this year.

**Jimmy Mullen**, *outside left (38 League appearances, 7 goals in 1953/54).*
On the left wing of Wolves' famous teams of the 1950s was the great Jimmy Mullen. Born in Newcastle-upon-Tyne on 6 January 1923, this affable Geordie joined Wolves in the summer of 1937. In his Wolves career he made 486 appearances, scoring 112 goals plus 28 goals from 89 games during the war. Jimmy also won 12 full England caps, scoring 6 goals. He made his Wolves debut on 18 February 1939 against Leeds United at the tender age of 16 years and 43 days, in a 4-1 win at Molineux. Jimmy was a member of Wolves' 1942 Wartime League North Cup-winning team, before playing a major role in winning 3 League Championships and the FA Cup. On the international scene, he scored against Switzerland in the 1954 World Cup finals, and had the distinction of being England's first ever substitute against Belgium in Brussels in 1950. He scored 15 minutes after coming on to replace Stan Mortenson. Jimmy Mullen also played in 3 wartime internationals, and for the England B and Football League sides. He died in October 1987 aged 64, a true gentleman in every sense of the word; a great loss.

**Eddie Stuart**, *right-back (12 League appearances in 1953/54).*
South African Eddie Stuart was born in Johannesburg on 12 May 1931, and made his Wolves debut as centre forward against Albion at Molineux on 15 April 1952, scoring in a 4-1 defeat. On a trip home in 1952 he contracted a career-threatening mystery illness, from which he fortunately recovered to play a massive role in Wolves' glory years. It was largely due to this illness that he didn't get a first-team game in the following season, and it was February 1954 before we saw him again in a League match, this time in the number two shirt which, apart from injuries, he pretty much made his own from then on. Stuart also sometimes played at centre half, and had the distinction of captaining Wolves against his home country in the inaugural floodlit match at Molineux in 1953; Bill Shorthouse stood down so that the young man could have this honour. In a long and distinguished career Eddie Stuart made 322 appearances for Wolves, scoring his only Wolves goal on his debut as centre forward against West Bromwich Albion. Eddie was another who was left out of Wolves 1960 FA Cup final line-up. He transferred to Stoke City in July 1962 for a fee of around £8,000 before moving on to Tranmere Rovers in 1964 and then to Stockport County. He ended his playing career as player/manager of Worcester City in 1970.

**Ron Flowers**, *left half, inside right and centre forward (15 League appearances in 1953/54).*
Ron Flowers was born in Edlington, South Yorkshire on 28 July 1934. Another product of Wath Wanderers, Ron joined Wolves in the summer of 1950, turning professional in 1952. He made his League debut at Molineux against Blackpool in a 5-2 defeat on 20 September 1952, playing at centre half. Ron Flowers went on to play 512 first-team games for Wolves, scoring 37 goals, winning 3 Championships and 1 FA Cup. The first of his 49 England Caps came in 1955, the last 11 years

later: a true testimony to the ability and longevity of this wonderful wing half. In the summer of 1962 it was World Cup final time once again; this time Chile were the hosts. Ron Flowers was the only Wolves representative to play in these finals, and distinguished his performances with goals from the penalty spot in each of England's first two group games, becoming the first non-forward to score in four successive internationals. England lost 2-1 to Hungary in their opening game, beat Argentina 3-1, and drew 0-0 with Bulgaria to reach the quarter-finals, where sadly they faced the holders Brazil, losing 3-1. When England hosted the 1966 World Cup finals Ron Flowers was selected for the England squad, but sadly didn't play in any of England's games. Ron won his 49th and final full cap on 29 June 1966 against Norway in Oslo. In September 1967, the last of Wolves' great players of the title-winning era left the club to join Northampton Town, where he later became player/coach before moving to Telford United as player/manager until 1971. Just about everyone in Wolverhampton knows Ron's sports shop in Queen Street.

Wath Wanderers was an amateur club from Wath-on-Dearne in Yorkshire which Major Frank Buckley took on as a feeder club for Wolves. Run by former Wolves player Mark Crook, this little club produced a number of promising players in what Buckley recognised as being a hugely cost-effective way of finding and blooding players. Revolutionary in its day, the idea has since been adopted by many top clubs. Along with Ron Flowers, Wath Wanderers produced John Short, Roy Swinbourne, Peter Knowles, Alan Sunderland and Steve Daley, to name a few.

The reserves:
**Nigel Sims**, *goalkeeper (8 League appearances in 1953.54).*
Born in Cotton-in-the-Elms, Derbyshire. As understudy to Bert Williams, Nigel Sims got few first-team opportunities following his debut at Sheffield United on 18 April 1949. He transferred to Aston Villa on 6 March 1956, after making only 39 appearances for Wolves. With Villa he won an FA Cup winners medal in 1957. Sims won 1 cap with Young England in 1953/54, and also played for the Army.
**Len Gibbons**, *right-back (1 League appearance in 1953/54).*
Len Gibbons hailed from Stan Cullis' birthplace, Ellesmere Port. He joined Wolves in 1951/52, making his League debut at left-back at Portsmouth on 15 September 1951, going on to make a total of 29 appearances for Wolves before leaving Molineux during Wolves' first Championship-winning season.

**Bill Guttridge**, *left-back (2 League appearances in 1953/54).*
Wolves' left-back on a number of occasions was hard as nails. Bill 'Chopper' Guttridge, when he managed to curb his sometimes overly aggressive style of play, turned in some first-class performances. Mind you, the fans loved to watch him play his natural game. He was a real crowd favourite,. This Darlaston-born lad made his debut at Aston Villa on Christmas Day 1951, making 2 appearances in each of 3 seasons before leaving the club to join Walsall Town, where he established himself once again as a favourite of the fans.

**Bill Baxter**, *right half (5 League appearances in 1953/54).*
Scottish born wing half Bill Baxter had many a good game for Wolves after making his debut on 4

December 1948 at Molineux against Everton. In all he made 47 appearances for Wolves, scoring 1 goal before transferring to Aston Villa on 26 November 1953.

**Norman Deeley**, *right half, left half and inside right (6 League appearances in 1953/54).*
Little Norman Deeley was born in Wednesbury on 30 November 1933 and went on to play for England Schoolboys. Norman was a little taller than Johnny Hancocks, and started out as a wing-half before switching to the wing to eventually take Johnny's place. Norman made his debut against Arsenal at Molineux on 25 August 1951, although it was not until 1957 that he established a claim to a regular first-team place. He went on to win 2 full England caps against Brazil and Peru, and for Wolves made 237 appearances, scoring 75 goals, including 2 in the 1960 FA Cup success against Blackburn Rovers at Wembley. Equally at home on either flank, Deeley's characteristic style of running – chin forward, chest out – was sorely missed when, in February 1962, he was transferred to Leyton Orient for £12,000.

**Ron Stockin**, *inside right and inside left (6 League appearances in 1953/54).*
Hailing from Walsall, Ronnie Stockin found it difficult to regularly break into Wolves' first eleven. He made his debut in January 1953, but was restricted to a total of 21 appearances, scoring 7 goals, before transferring to Cardiff City in 1953/54.

**Les Smith**, *outside left and outside right (4 League appearances, 1 goal in 1953/54).*
Long-serving winger Les Smith joined Wolves on amateur forms in June 1945, making his League Division One debut on 17 April 1948 in the 3-2 away win at Stoke City. Born in Halesowen on 24 December 1927, he was another who found it hard to establish himself as a first-choice winger at Molineux. His best season was 1954/55, when he made 34 League plus 4 Cup appearances deputising for both Hancocks and Mullen, scoring 6 League goals, plus 1 in the Cup. In total he made 94 appearances for Wolves, scoring 24 goals. On 2 February 1956, he joined Aston Villa for a fee of £25,000, where he established himself as a top-class right-winger, winning an FA Cup winners medal in 1957. Sadly, in 1960, an Achilles tendon injury halted his career after only 130 appearances for Villa, in which time he scored 25 goals.

**Eddie Clamp**, *left half and inside left (2 League appearances in 1953/54).*
Nicknamed 'Chopper' by a large section of the fans because of his often uncompromising style of play, Eddie went on to become a hero on the terraces at Molineux. I remember one powerful shoulder-charge on Albion's darling Johnny Nicholls, when Clamp knocked the WBA starlet off the pitch, lifting him high in the air and into the crowd in the Molineux Street Paddock; Eddie stood no messing that was sure. However, his hard-man image sometimes belied the skill that he definitely possessed; you weren't selected for England if you couldn't play. Eddie Clamp won 4 full England caps, all in 1958 as part of England's all-Wolves half-back line with Billy Wright and Bill Slater. Eddie was born in Coalville, Leicestershire on 14 September 1943, joining Wolves groundstaff in 1949 and making his debut at Old Trafford on 6 March 1954. For Wolves, he made 241 appearances, scoring 25 goals in a career that saw him win 2 First Division Championship medals plus 1 for the FA Cup in 1960. Eddie Clamp was transferred to Arsenal in November 1961 for a

huge £35,000 fee, moving on to Stoke City in September 1962. He later joined Peterborough United and Worcester City, before ending his career with Lower Gornal in 1969.

**Ray Chatham**, *right half (1 League appearance in 1953/54).*
Local boy Ray Chatham was born in Wolverhampton on 20 July 1924, signing amateur forms for Wolves during the Second World War, making his debut at the start of the 1945/46 season at centre forward and scoring 16 goals in 32 wartime League and FA Cup games. The opportunities for this utility player, who in 1946/47 had moved into the half-back line, were fairly restricted, with the majority of his 86 appearances coming at centre half, scoring 2 goals in his Wolves first-team career. In January 1954 he moved to Notts County.

Dennis Wilshaw's goal against Birmingham City in the FA Cup gave him an overall total for the season of 27, putting him fourth place in the League scoring charts. Johnny Hancocks and Roy Swinbourne also made the top ten. The Black Country domination of the list was enforced with Ronnie Allen's 27 League plus 7 Cup goals, and Johnny Nicholls 28 League plus 4 Cup goals.

Additionally, Wolves scored 8 goals in the 3 floodlit friendlies played in 1953/54: Mullen and Wilshaw got 2 each; Swinbourne, Broadbent, Taylor and Deeley all weighed in with 1 apiece.

Two other players played a part in the 1953/54 season; although not in the League:

#### Bobby Mason
Slightly-built Tipton lad Bobby Mason was seventeen years old when he was given the chance to make his debut for the first team in the floodlit friendly against Glasgow Celtic on 14 October 1953 (details earlier in the book). Born on 22 March 1936, inside forward Bobby Mason first signed for Wolves as an amateur, making his League debut in November 1955, before going on to score 54 goals in 173 games, winning Championship medals in 1957/58 and 1958/59. One of the burning, and as far as I know, unanswered questions, is why did Stan Cullis really leave him out of Wolves' FA Cup-winning team in 1960 in favour of eighteen-year-old Barry Stobart? Stobart got his chance in Wolves' final game of the 1959/60 season against Chelsea, doing well in a 5-1 win, so maybe it was just a case of preferring the younger man. Mason had virtually been ever-present in the side that season, playing in 37 League games, scoring 13 (although 11 of these were netted before Christmas), only missing a few games through injury. Mason played in every round of the Cup except the final, scoring twice in the 6 games; both in the fifth-round victory at Luton. He had also played in all 6 European matches, scoring 4 goals, the last on 2 March against Barcelona. The final part of the mystery is that Bobby Mason retained his place in the starting line-up for the following season's campaign, scoring 6 in 28 games, with Stobart no more than a reserve player. In May 1962 Mason was transferred to Leyton Orient for £10,000.

#### Doug Taylor
Young centre forward Doug Taylor got his chance of first-team action in the third floodlit friendly at Molineux against Racing Club of Buenos Aires on 10 March 1954, in which he scored the first of Wolves' 3 goals. Doug made his League debut at Villa Park on 12 April 1955 in a 4-2 defeat, the first of 3 consecutive appearances. He never again played for the first team, and moved on to Walsall Town.

# 1953/54 Statistics

Summary of League Appearances:

42 – Johnny Hancocks.

40 – Bill Shorthouse, Roy Swinbourne.

39 – Bill Slater, Billy Wright, Dennis Wilshaw.

38 – Jimmy Mullen.

36 – Peter Broadbent.

34 – Bert Williams.

27 – Roy Pritchard.

26 – John Short.

15 – Ron Flowers.

12 – Eddie Stuart.

8 – Nigel Sims.

6 – Norman Deeley, Ron Stockin (transferred to Cardiff City).

5 – Bill Baxter (transferred to Aston Villa).

4 – Les Smith.

2 – Bill Guttridge, Eddie Clamp.

1 – Len Gibbons, Ray Chatham (transferred to Notts County).

The League Goal-scorers:

26 – Dennis Wilshaw, plus 1 in the FA Cup.

24 – Johnny Hancocks, including 5 penalties.

24 – Roy Swinbourne.

12 – Peter Broadbent.

7 – Jimmy Mullen.

2 – Bill Slater.

1 – Les Smith.

A total of 96 League goals.

3 hat-tricks were scored, all at Molineux:

Dennis Wilshaw in the 4-3 victory over Portsmouth.

Johnny Hancocks in the 8-1 annihilation of Chelsea.

Roy Swinbourne in the 4-1 humbling of Blackpool.

Wolves' first-team squad.

The backroom staff:

**Stan Cullis**, *Manager*

Stan Cullis was born in Ellesmere Port, Cheshire on 25 October 1915, joining Wolves in February 1934, making his debut at right half on 16 February 1935 in a 3-2 defeat at Molineux. He was a great centre half, tough-tackling, good in the air, and a shrewd and thoughtful passer of the ball. A born leader, he captained Wolves before his nineteenth birthday, and England a few years later. The outbreak of war restricted him to 12 full England caps plus 20 wartime international appearances. He was a member of Wolves' losing FA Cup final team in 1939, when the popular opinion was that Wolves only had to turn up to win; Portsmouth beat them 4-1. When the great man prematurely hung up his boots in May 1947 after making 171 appearances for Wolves, he surprised most pundits. Stan then accepted the post of assistant manager to Ted Vizard, and at age thirty-two he became the youngest man to manage at this level. A year later, on 23 June 1948, he took over as manager of Wolves, to begin an era of success. As the architect of Wolves' triumphs, his record as manager was 3 League Championships, in 1953/54, 57/58 and 58/59, and two FA Cups, in 1949 and 1960, the year Wolves almost won the double, finishing as runners-up by 1 point to Burnley.

Stan Cullis was a tough, uncompromising and inspirational manager who steered Wolves to the most successful period in their history. In 1947/48 Wolves ended the season in fifth spot, and a year later in 1948/49 achieved sixth position, also winning the FA Cup that season. In 1949/50 Wolves were runners-up in both League and Cup, their second spot in the League equalling the highest finish that they had thus far achieved in their history, matching as it did the 2 runners-up finishes in the two seasons before the outbreak of war. Not winning the title that season was a bitter pill to swallow, as Portsmouth only won the Championship on goal difference, both teams having 53 points. Over the course of the next two seasons Wolves' form dipped considerably, falling to 14th position in 1950/51, and in 1951/52 ending the season in 16th spot. The following season, 1952/53, saw a resurgence of Wolves' fortunes as they once again claimed third place. In 10 seasons, excluding the war break, Wolves had finished second 3 times, 2 third placings, 2 fifth placings and a sixth place finish, and won the FA Cup once, to earn the recognition as being among the top clubs in the country. Then of course came Wolves' first League Championship. Responding to a number of unkind and tactically challenged critics who had branded Wolves' style of play 'Kick and Rush', Stan Cullis reportedly announced, 'Our forwards are not encouraged to parade their ability in ostentatious fashion! The longer the ball is in our opponent's goal area, the more chances we will have to score!' You couldn't argue with Stan's sentiments; the proof was there for all to see, in the trophies that Wolves won.

Stan Cullis' full managerial record in 16 years at Wolves was:

FA Cup Winners – twice
First Division Champions – 3 times
Runners-up – 3 times
3rd place – 3 times
5th place – once
6th place – twice
14th – once

# 1953/54 Statistics

16th – twice
18th – once
Losing FA Cup semi-finalists – once
Total first-team games played under his management: 748, won 350, drew 171, lost 227.
Goals for: 1,563
Goals against: 1,162
Total League points: 792

Success under Stan Cullis wasn't restricted to the first eleven. Under his guidance, the reserves were Champions of the Central League 5 times, in 1950/51, 1951/52, 1952/53, 1957/58 and 1958/59. The youth team won the FA Youth Cup once, in 1957/58, and were beaten finalists on 3 other occasions, in 1952/53, 1953/54 and 1961/62.

In 1964, the fortunes of Cullis and Wolverhampton Wanderers took a distinct turn for the worse, as money-spinning European qualification now became just a dream. The team's performance got worse, culminating in relegation at the end of the 1964/65 season. The end of an era was about to shatter the lives of the fans. First, Chairman James Marshall handed over the reins to John Ireland. Then, two months later at the end of a long illness, the greatest Wolves manager of all time was sacked by the new chairman. This black day was 15 September 1964. The team had lost their first 3 matches, drawn the 4th, then proceeded to lose the next 3, so it was against the backdrop of this disastrous start (played 7, lost 6, drawn 1, points 1) that the knives were being sharpened for Stan. Attendances had also dropped significantly compared to that of their rivals; something had to give. In their 8th match, Wolves reversed the trend by beating West Ham 4-3 at Molineux; that was on 14 September 1964, the day before Cullis was forced to leave his beloved Wolves. For many years Stan Cullis was Wolverhampton Wanderers. A proud and dedicated man, he was one of the small breed of outstanding footballing giants, who achieved greatness both as a player and manager; even fewer have achieved both with the same club. The following year Stan Cullis was appointed manager of Birmingham City, where he stayed until March 1970. The great man has never been awarded the accolades that his achievements deserved. Now, with the unveiling of a statue of Stan sited outside the stand that bears his name, Wolves have rightly ensured that his memory will live on in the hearts and minds of all true Wolves fans. Stan Cullis passed away in February 2001. Football is all the poorer for his passing.

**Joe Gardiner**, *Trainer*
Left half Joe Gardiner was born in Bearpark, County Durham on 24 December 1911. Joining Wolves in 1932 on amateur forms, he made his debut in the 5-2 defeat at West Brom on February 1935. Joe went on to play 139 games for the first eleven, scoring 2 goals. He was a member of Wolves' losing Cup final team in 1939; however, the war curtailed his career, and he retired from playing in 1944, but stayed on to become first-team trainer.

The Directors:
In 1953 the Wolves board comprised:
   *Mr James Baker* – Chairman

*Mr Arthur H. Oakley, JP* – Vice-Chairman
*Mr James Evans*
*Mr Charles H. Hunter*
*Mr James H. Marshall*

In 1953, towards the end of what had been a particularly successful period in Wolves' history, and urged on by Stan Cullis, the forward-thinking Molineux board had taken the monumental decision to be among the first football League clubs to install floodlights, thus heralding a series of memorable night games. Wolves fans everywhere owe the board of directors of that time a huge debt of gratitude, because without their courage and vision we would have been deprived of the magnificent spectacles that were to follow.

**Jack Howley**, *Club Secretary*
Club Secretary Jack Howley started working for Wolves as office boy in 1923, and was appointed Secretary in June 1948, carrying out his duties through all the great Wolves years until he retired in June 1968 after forty-five years' service. For his last five years with Wolves he also acted as General Manager. Sadly, he died on 23 March 1971; a Wolves man through and through.

A number of other backroom boys should be mentioned before we close the annals on 1953/54: Chief Scout George Noakes, Physiotherapist George Palmer, Trainer Jack Dowen, Chief Scout George Poyser and Groundsman Albert Tye.

Wolves' backroom boys: From left to right: Stan Cullis, manager; Joe Gardiner, trainer; George Palmer, physiotherapist; Jack Dowen, trainer; and George Poyser, chief scout.

# Postscript

**England**
England played Yugoslavia in Belgrade on 16 May 1954 prior to travelling to Budapest for the return match with Hungary. They lost 1-0 with a team including Midlands players Gil Merrick, Billy Wright, Ronnie Allen, Johnny Nicholls and Jimmy Mullen. And of course, on 23 May 1954, they were murdered 7-1 by the Hungarians.

In the summer of 1954, Switzerland staged the World Cup finals and, fittingly, Champions Wolves provided a number of players for the England squad. Billy Wright captained England in both their group matches; against Belgium, which England won 4-3 after extra time with Billy the only Wolves player in that match, and against Switzerland, England winning 2-0 with Dennis Wilshaw and Jimmy Mullen joining their captain and scoring a goal apiece. Mullen stood in for Nat Lofthouse at centre forward. Unfortunately, in the quarter-finals, England lost 4-2 to Uruguay, Wright and Wilshaw making the starting line-up for that match.

It was at a meeting during the 1954 World Cup finals in Switzerland that UEFA was founded.

**Wolves**
So, that was Wolves' first Championship-winning season. Now they knew they could do it they couldn't wait to do it again. The following season, 1954/55, Wolves finished second, 4 points behind Chelsea. The season after that, 1955/56, they finished third behind Champions Manchester United and Blackpool Town. In 1956/57, Manchester United won the title again, with Wolves dropping into sixth place. Then of course came 1957/58 and Wolves' second League Championship, followed by 1958/59, when once again they were Champions, and 1959/60, when they won the FA Cup but disappointingly finished in the runners-up spot to Burnley by 1 point, thereby missing out on a League and Cup double. These were three glorious seasons. A fabulous decade of football riches – Wolverhampton Wanderers were the team of the 1950s, of that there is no doubt.

If you are interested in purchasing other books published by Tempus,
or in case you have difficulty finding any Tempus books in your local bookshop,
you can also place orders directly through our website
**www.tempus-publishing.com**